The Future of Pension Systems in Greece: The Role of Private Insurers in Light of Demographic Change

Dissertation | Applied Research in Pension Economics and Insurance

Thomas Rammopoulos

Doctor of Business Administration

Munich, 2026

FOREWORD

This work is a revised and expanded version of the doctoral dissertation submitted to VERN University (Zagreb) and the International Business Academy of Switzerland (IBAS) in May 2026 in partial fulfilment of the requirements for the award of the Doctor of Business Administration.

The revisions for this published edition address examiner feedback and expand the original submission in four respects. First, a standalone Executive Summary has been added to make the principal findings and policy conclusions accessible to a non-specialist audience. Second, a new chapter section on Practitioner Reflections (Section 5.10) provides a qualitative synthesis of the open-ended research dimensions that the quantitative analysis could not fully address. Third, the methodological presentation has been strengthened, including a documented literature search strategy and a more explicit acknowledgement of the temporal scope limitations associated with the long-run research horizon. Fourth, the reference list has been completed to include all sources cited in the text.

The substantive argument, empirical findings, and conclusions of the original dissertation remain unchanged. The research was conducted independently under the supervision of Dr. Hatem Haggag, and the author retains full responsibility for all content. The dissertation was assessed and accepted by both awarding institutions in May 2026.

Thomas Rammopoulos, DBA

Munich, June 2026

EXECUTIVE SUMMARY

Background and Purpose

Greece faces one of the most acute pension sustainability challenges in the European Union. Its public pay-as-you-go system, already strained by a decade of fiscal adjustment and repeated reform, now confronts the structural pressure of sustained demographic ageing. The old-age dependency ratio is projected to rise sharply through 2050, while the contribution base continues to shrink. Against this background, the central question addressed in this dissertation is not whether reform is necessary, but how a more balanced and financially resilient pension architecture can realistically be constructed. In particular, the study examines the potential contribution of private insurers within a developing multi-pillar framework, and the conditions under which supplementary pension provision can strengthen retirement income security without replacing the public system.

Research Approach

This dissertation takes a practice-oriented approach consistent with applied doctoral research. It draws on a structured survey of 68 stakeholders with professional exposure to pension policy, insurance, and related fields, including pension experts, insurance professionals, policymakers, economists, and public servants. The empirical analysis combines descriptive statistics, reliability testing, correlation analysis, independent samples t-tests, and regression modelling. These methods are used to identify how practitioners perceive the sustainability and adequacy of the current Greek pension system, and under what conditions they view private insurer involvement as a credible and beneficial development.

Principal Findings

The findings reveal limited confidence in the long-term sustainability of the current Greek pension system, with a mean sustainability rating of 2.53 on a five-point scale. Respondents are equally sceptical about adequacy, rating the current system's ability to meet future retirement needs at 2.28. These low scores establish a clear empirical foundation for the dissertation's central argument: the present structure cannot be assumed to remain viable under projected demographic conditions without meaningful structural adjustment.

Demographic pressure is recognised as the primary structural constraint. The items measuring perceived ageing pressure and expected future demographic strain receive the highest means in the dataset, at 4.34 and 4.31 respectively. This is an important finding. It indicates that practitioners do not view the pension challenge as temporary or cyclical, but as a long-term structural condition that existing reform measures have not fully addressed.

Support for private insurer involvement is broadly positive but explicitly conditional. Respondents assign a mean importance score of 4.01 to the role of private insurers, and they place the highest priority in the entire dataset on the need for simple and transparent product design, with a mean of 4.43. This result speaks directly to RQ3. It suggests that practitioners do not endorse private provision as an abstract market solution. Rather, they see it as a credible supplement to the public system only where governance quality, consumer protection, and product clarity are effectively ensured.

The correlation analysis reinforces this picture. Perceived demographic pressure is positively associated with support for tax reform ($r = 0.489$, $p < 0.01$) and income diversification ($r = 0.488$, $p < 0.01$). Perceived insurer importance is strongly correlated with the view that private insurance is essential to address adequacy gaps ($r = 0.621$, $p < 0.01$). These associations indicate that practitioners connect demographic concern with reform orientation rather than passive acceptance, and that support for private provision is embedded in a broader view of what a more resilient pension system should look like.

Policy Implications

The findings carry several concrete implications for policymakers, insurance-sector decision-makers, and regulatory bodies. For policymakers, the evidence points to an urgent need to reform tax incentives for private pension savings, strengthen consumer protection legislation, and explore auto-enrolment mechanisms that reduce reliance on voluntary participation alone. The strong practitioner support for auto-enrolment (mean = 3.93) and tax reform (mean = 4.24) indicates that these measures would be viewed as credible and workable rather than simply aspirational.

For insurance-sector decision-makers, the study identifies product simplicity, longevity risk management, and governance transparency as the conditions under which market expansion is both feasible and legitimate. Insurers that invest in accessible, clearly structured products with independently verifiable performance records are better positioned to build the client trust that Greece's supplementary market currently lacks. For regulatory bodies, including EIOPA and national supervisors, the findings support a more active coordination role in ensuring that the framework conditions for supplementary provision are not only technically sound but also publicly credible.

Overall Conclusion

This dissertation does not argue that private insurers can resolve Greece's pension challenge. The evidence does not support that conclusion. What it does show is that a carefully governed, transparency-oriented supplementary tier can meaningfully complement the public system, and that the conditions under which this is possible are knowable, measurable, and to a significant degree achievable. The path forward requires coordinated action across institutional, regulatory, and market dimensions. It is neither straightforward nor guaranteed. But the evidence presented in this study suggests that it is both necessary and, under the right conditions, realistic.

ABSTRACT

This dissertation investigates the sustainability and future adequacy of the Greek pension system under the combined pressures of demographic ageing and fiscal limitation. Greece remains one of the European cases where pension provision is still predominantly organised through a public pay-as-you-go structure, while long-term demographic projections indicate a steadily shrinking contribution base.

The central question is therefore not whether reform is necessary, but how a more balanced structure could realistically be achieved. In this context, particular attention is given to the potential contribution of private insurers within a gradually developing multi-pillar framework. The analysis does not assume that private provision offers a substitute for the public system. Instead, it examines under which institutional and regulatory conditions supplementary mechanisms may enhance retirement income security.

The empirical component draws on survey data from 68 professionally relevant stakeholders in pensions, insurance, and policy-related fields. The methodological approach includes descriptive evaluation, internal consistency testing, correlation analysis, independent samples t-tests, and regression modelling. These methods allow for the identification of perceived sustainability risks, adequacy concerns, and conditional support patterns.

The findings point to limited confidence in the long-term resilience of the current system and strong recognition of demographic ageing as a structural constraint. Support for private insurers emerges primarily in relation to adequacy and longevity-risk management, but it is closely tied to governance quality, transparency, and effective consumer safeguards. The evidence therefore suggests complementarity rather than substitution.

Overall, the dissertation integrates demographic, fiscal, behavioural, and governance dimensions into a practice-oriented analytical framework specific to the Greek institutional environment. The conclusions are intended to inform both policymakers and insurance-sector decision-makers concerned with strengthening supplementary pension provision while preserving systemic stability and public trust.

TABLE OF CONTENTS

LIST OF ABBREVIATIONS

DC	Defined Contribution
EU	European Union
EIOPA	European Insurance and Occupational Pensions Authority
ELSTAT	Hellenic Statistical Authority
GDP	Gross Domestic Product
HICP	Harmonised Index of Consumer Prices
IMF	International Monetary Fund
NDC	Notional Defined Contribution
OADR	Old-Age Dependency Ratio
OECD	Organisation for Economic Co-operation and Development
PAYG	Pay-As-You-Go
PEPP	Pan-European Personal Pension Product
Q2	Second Quarter
RRP	Recovery and Resilience Plan
TFR	Total Fertility Rate
TEKA	Auxiliary Defined Contribution Pension Fund of Greece (Ταμείο Επικουρικής Κεφαλαιοποιητικής Ασφάλισης)

LIST OF TABLES

LIST OF FIGURES

Chapter 1 INTRODUCTION & IMPORTANCE

1.1 Introduction

This dissertation looks at the sustainability challenges facing the Greek pension system in the context of demographic ageing, long-standing fiscal constraints, and repeated reform efforts. As the population ages, pressure on pay-as-you-go pension systems has increased across Europe. In Greece, this pressure has been particularly strong due to the economic crisis and the limited fiscal room available to support public pension provision.

Although a series of pension reforms has been implemented over the past decades, the public pension system remains the central pillar of old-age income in Greece. These reforms have helped stabilise public finances in the short and medium term, but they have not fully resolved the underlying tensions between sustainability, benefit adequacy, and public acceptance. As a result, the question of how supplementary pension arrangements can contribute to future retirement income has become increasingly relevant.

From a practical and managerial point of view, this creates a clear challenge. Policymakers and regulators have to decide whether additional pension mechanisms can be added to the existing system without weakening public trust or putting too much risk on individuals. At the same time, private insurers face limits of their own, including regulation, product design, market capacity, and long-term risk management. Any realistic discussion of their role therefore has to look at both the opportunities and the limits.

This study is part of a Doctor of Business Administration (DBA) programme and takes an applied, practice-oriented approach. It does not aim to build abstract theory. Instead, it seeks to generate insights that are relevant for decision-makers in public institutions and in the insurance sector. The study looks at the conditions under which private insurers may contribute to a multi-pillar pension system in Greece and at the factors that may limit such a role.

This chapter sets out the background and context of the study, defines the research problem, and presents the objectives and research questions used in the analysis. It also outlines the scope and structure of the dissertation and provides the framework for the chapters that follow.

1.2 Research Background

1.2.1. Historical and Institutional Background

The sustainability of pension systems has become a major policy issue across Europe, and Greece is one of the clearest and most complex cases. Historically, the Greek pension system was characterised by fragmentation, strong reliance on pay-as-you-go financing, dependence on public provision, and only limited development of supplementary private pension arrangements. Before the global financial crisis, generous replacement rates, early-retirement incentives, and weak links between contributions and benefits contributed to rising fiscal pressure and broader structural imbalances within the system.

Before the sovereign debt crisis, Greece developed a pension system that combined strong public dominance with high institutional fragmentation. The system operated through numerous occupation-based funds and special regimes, and it often delivered relatively generous replacement rates while permitting early retirement pathways for multiple categories of workers (Nektarios & Tinios, 2019). This structure weakened transparency and blurred the contribution–benefit link, which increased inequities across groups and reduced incentives for long contribution histories. Over time, these design features amplified fiscal exposure in a pay-as-you-go setting and created structural vulnerabilities that macroeconomic shocks later revealed more sharply (Kangur et al., 2021).

The sovereign debt crisis that began in 2009 marked a major turning point for the Greek pension system. Under international financial assistance programmes, Greece introduced a wide range of reforms aimed at restoring fiscal sustainability. These included benefit cuts, higher retirement ages, contribution base reforms, and the consolidation of pension funds (Chrysanthopoulou et al., 2023). Although these measures improved fiscal outcomes in the short and medium term, they also exposed the structural limits of a pension model that remained heavily dependent on public financing, especially in the face of adverse demographic trends such as population ageing, falling birth rates, and rising old-age dependency ratios (Konstantinidou & Koumarianos, 2025).

After 2009, Greece entered a longer period of pension reform that aimed to restore affordability, simplify governance, and reduce fragmentation. Policymakers introduced successive parametric and structural measures, including pension benefit cuts, increases in statutory and effective retirement ages, revisions to indexation and accrual rules, and repeated fund consolidation. Reforms in the mid-2010s also strengthened unification and harmonisation by reducing legacy distortions and moving administration towards a more centralised model. This improved fiscal indicators, but it also triggered debates about distribution and adequacy (Kangur et al., 2021). The literature shows that this period was shaped not only by consolidation and cost containment, but also by significant implementation difficulties and social tension. Households had to adjust to repeated pension cuts and to an environment marked by uncertainty, which affected both consumption behaviour and confidence in long-term pension commitments (Laliotis et al., 2023).

Against this background, policy debates in Greece have gradually shifted toward the idea of a more diversified pension structure. Rather than relying exclusively on the public pay-as-you-go pillar, recent reform initiatives and policy proposals have explored the strengthening of funded components, the encouragement of private pension schemes, and a more structured involvement of private insurers in retirement provision (Bravo, Ayuso, and Mekkaoui, 2025). At the same time, there is no consensus that such approaches automatically improve sustainability or adequacy. Their impact depends heavily on regulatory design, market depth, risk allocation, and the extent to which social protection objectives are preserved (Glette-Iversen, Flage, and Aven, 2023).

These questions are particularly relevant in the Greek case, where demographic pressure, fiscal constraints, institutional trust, and market capacity interact. The dissertation therefore examines the sustainability challenges of the Greek pension system and the role of private insurers as potential complementary actors within a multi-pillar framework, while recognising the institutional, regulatory, and market conditions that shape such a role.

The Greek pension system is increasingly shaped by long-term demographic and fiscal pressures that are common across European welfare states but particularly pronounced in the Greek case. Declining fertility rates and rising life expectancy have led to rapid population ageing, placing sustained pressure on contribution-based social insurance systems that were designed for a more favourable demographic structure (European Commission, 2024; World Bank, 2022). Greece is among the most rapidly ageing societies in Europe and continues to record persistently low fertility rates. These demographic developments have gradually altered the ratio between contributors and beneficiaries in the public pension system, increasing the structural demands placed on pay-as-you-go financing arrangements (OECD, 2024).

World Bank data show that Greece's old-age dependency ratio reached about 36 people aged 65 and over for every 100 people of working age in 2022, and the projections suggest that this trend will continue in the coming decades (World Bank, 2022). As Figure 1.1 shows, this is part of a broader demographic shift rather than a short-term fluctuation (European Commission, 2024). In a pension system that still relies mainly on pay-as-you-go financing, changes of this kind place growing pressure on the balance between contributions and pension obligations. Over time, this can mean higher contribution rates, greater support from the state, or further adjustments to pension benefits (OECD, 2024a).

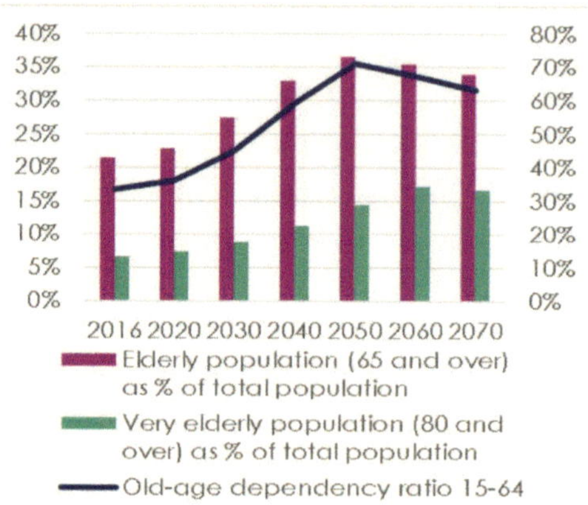

Figure 1.1 Old-age dependency ratio in Greece. Source: World Bank (2022)

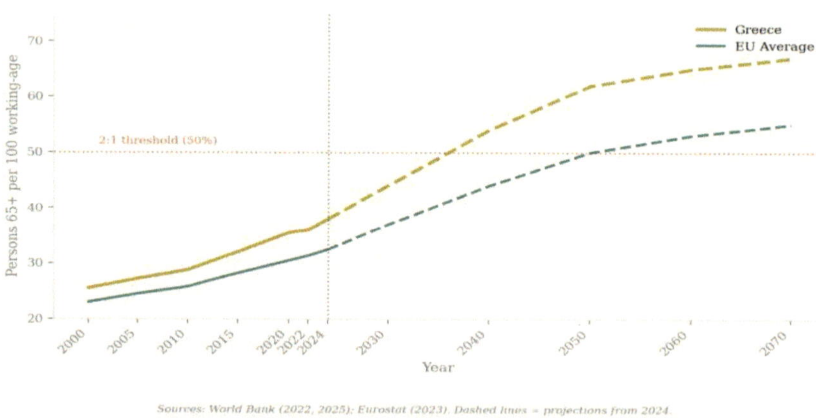

Figure 1.2 Old-age dependency ratio, Greece and EU average. Source: World Bank (2023,2025); Eurostat (2023)

This trend also has an important fiscal side, especially in Greece. Pension spending has historically taken up a relatively large share of GDP, while fiscal capacity has remained limited in the period after the sovereign debt crisis. Public pension expenditure has remained above the European Union average for long periods (European Commission, 2024). Although successive reforms have improved some indicators of sustainability, concerns still remain about the long-term adequacy of pensions and about whether the system can cope with further demographic pressure (OECD, 2024).

1.2.2. Research Context

Greece's pension system has evolved through repeated reform waves and processes of institutional consolidation. The Ageing Report fiche describes a system centred on e-EFKA, which administers main pensions, auxiliary provision, and additional benefits for selected professional categories, alongside means-tested support for uninsured elderly persons. It also highlights TEKA as the newly introduced auxiliary defined contribution (DC) scheme for many new labour market entrants from 2022 onward (European Commission, 2024). This institutional shift signals a gradual move towards funded, individual-account elements within the auxiliary pillar, while the main pension remains predominantly financed on a pay-as-you-go (PAYG) basis.

The wider European context reinforces the relevance of supplementary pensions. The OECD observes that funded pension assets have expanded across member countries and can contribute meaningfully to retirement security when governance structures are robust, fees are transparent, and investment risk is managed appropriately over the life cycle (OECD, 2024a). At the same time, supplementary pension provision in Europe remains uneven. Research and audit evidence document a strong concentration of occupational pension assets in a limited number of Member States, reflecting differences in labour market structures, institutional capacity, and historical development paths (Guardiancich & Natali, 2011).

A practical indicator of Greece's current scale in funded pensions is the size of occupational pension funds. According to a Bank of Greece release, total assets of occupational pension funds increased to €2,639 million at the end of the second quarter of 2025, up from €2,543 million in the previous quarter (Bank of Greece, 2025). While this growth is positive, it also underscores the relatively small size of Greece's funded pillar when compared to the footprint of the public pension system.

Regulation and product design play a central role in determining whether funded pensions can expand further. Supervisory and audit evidence points to persistent barriers to cross-border personal pensions, including weak participation incentives, fragmented national tax treatment, and limited provider engagement in the Pan-European Personal Pension Product (PEPP) framework (EIOPA, 2024). For Greece, this implies that private insurers can contribute meaningfully only if national policy choices—such as tax incentives, enrolment features, disclosure standards, and consumer protection rules—support long-term saving and foster credibility.

Within this institutional and regulatory setting, private insurers can contribute in several complementary ways. They may offer funded personal pension products that accumulate retirement assets and diversify income sources beyond public benefits. They can also provide decumulation products, such as lifetime annuities, that address longevity risk and reduce the likelihood that individuals exhaust their savings in old age. In addition, insurers can function as long-term institutional investors capable of matching long-duration liabilities with diversified asset portfolios. However, the effectiveness of these contributions depends critically on trust, product simplicity, and strong governance, as households frequently face decision frictions in retirement planning and decumulation choices (de Andrés-Sánchez & Puchades, 2025; OECD, 2024).

1.2.3. Studied Industry

Greece constitutes a particularly relevant case because retirement provision remains heavily concentrated in the public pay-as-you-go pension system, while funded pensions and private insurance play a limited, though gradually expanding, role. Despite repeated pension reforms and the recent introduction of funded auxiliary arrangements, private and occupational pensions account for only a small share of total retirement resources. This imbalance raises questions about the capacity of private insurance to complement public provision in a system historically designed around public redistribution rather than market-based savings.

The importance of this industry is closely linked to demographic developments. Greece is experiencing rapid population ageing as a result of persistently low fertility rates, rising life expectancy, and the emigration of working-age individuals. These trends increase financial pressure on public pension schemes and intensify concerns regarding both the sustainability and adequacy of future pensions. In this context, the potential contribution of funded pensions and private insurance to retirement security becomes a central issue rather than a marginal one.

Private insurers operate at the intersection of long-term saving, risk pooling, and capital market investment. In principle, they are well placed to address longevity risk and to provide stable income streams during retirement. In practice, however, their role is shaped by regulatory design, tax treatment, consumer confidence, and limited participation. Analysing the pension system and private insurance sector as an integrated industry, therefore, provides insight into how demographic change, institutional constraints, and market structures jointly influence retirement outcomes in Greece.

1.3 Importance of the Study

The study matters for policymakers because Greece must manage a difficult trade-off between fiscal sustainability and pension adequacy. Pension spending remains large relative to the size of the economy and interacts with other policy goals, including economic growth, healthcare financing, and social inclusion. For context, Eurostat reports that pension expenditure across the European Union averaged 12.2% of GDP in 2022 (Eurostat, 2025). Greece's pension expenditure of 14.5% of GDP in the same year, therefore, signals above-average fiscal pressure and highlights why pension system design shapes broader economic policy choices (Eurostat, 2025).

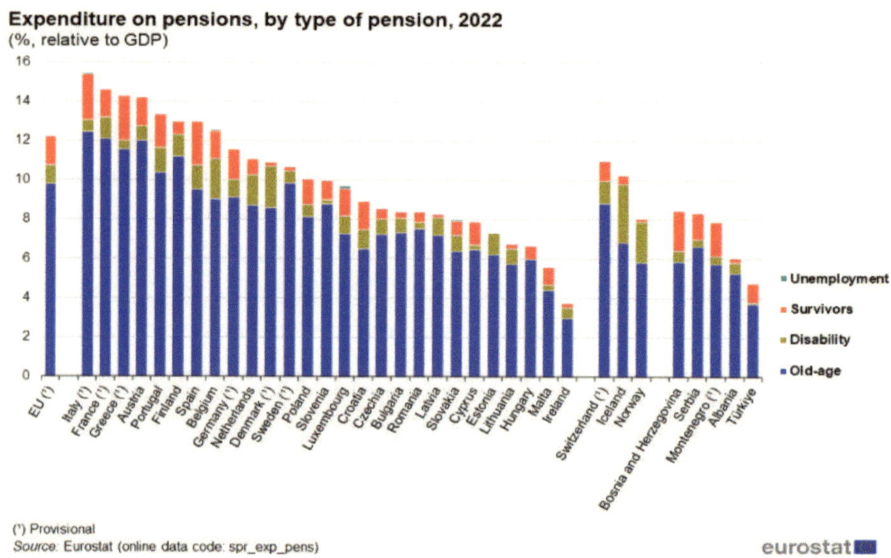

Figure 1.3 Pension Expenditure across the EU. Source: Eurostat (2025)

The study also matters for insurance executives and pension managers because population ageing alters both demand conditions and risk profiles. Longer retirement periods increase demand for products that provide stable and predictable income streams, while simultaneously raising insurers' exposure to longevity risk, reinvestment risk, and inflation uncertainty. Recent research frequently discusses lifetime annuities in connection with longevity risk. While these products are often presented as an effective hedge against the financial consequences of longer life expectancy, empirical evidence suggests that households tend to perceive them as complex and sometimes difficult to evaluate. This perception appears to affect participation decisions and highlights the importance of transparency, disclosure standards, and accessible financial advice (Hanbali, 2024; Wan et al., 2025).

In the Greek context, longevity risk is not a theoretical concern. Demographic projections indicate a steady rise in the population aged 80 and above, increasing from approximately 7% in 2016 to an estimated 14% by 2050 (World Bank, 2020; Kyriopoulos et al., 2025). Longer retirement periods are likely to coincide with higher healthcare and long-term care needs. Private insurance mechanisms may help households stabilise income in later life, but this depends on pricing fairness and effective regulatory safeguards. Although annuities can pool longevity risk efficiently, demand tends to remain limited where products are seen as expensive or difficult to understand (De Andrés-Sánchez & Puchades, 2025).

The issue also matters at European Union level, since Greece does not operate in a purely national pension environment. Its pension market is shaped by a wider regulatory framework and by EU-level initiatives. The European Court of Auditors has noted that EU action has so far had limited success in strengthening occupational pensions and has not led to the broad uptake of the Pan-European Personal Pension Product (PEPP) (European Court of Auditors, 2025). This wider setting affects what is realistically possible for both national pension reform and private providers.

The study is also intended to address a practical decision-making problem. For policymakers, regulators, and senior managers in the insurance sector, the central issue is not whether private insurers can play any role at all, but under which conditions that role can expand without weakening pension adequacy or public trust.

For practitioners, the findings are relevant to questions of product design, governance, and regulatory alignment in supplementary pension provision.

From a policy perspective, they also help clarify which institutional and market constraints continue to shape the feasible role of private insurance within a multi-pillar system.

The importance of this study also extends beyond the Greek case itself. Greece provides a particularly relevant setting because it combines rapid demographic ageing, constrained fiscal capacity, repeated reform experience, and still limited development of supplementary pension provision. In that sense, it can be viewed as a useful case for examining wider questions that affect other European welfare states as well. These include how far public pension systems can absorb long-term demographic pressure on their own, under what conditions funded supplementary arrangements can expand, and how trust, governance, and regulatory design shape the role of private providers. The study is therefore relevant not only for understanding pension reform in Greece, but also for broader debates about how ageing societies can balance sustainability, adequacy, and institutional legitimacy over time.

1.4 Research Problem, Objectives, and Questions

1.4.1. Research Problem

Greece must sustain adequate pensions under conditions of rapid demographic ageing while maintaining fiscal stability and public trust. The projected rise in the old-age dependency ratio increases pressure on pay-as-you-go (PAYG) financing and raises the likelihood of repeated policy adjustments over time (World Bank, 2020). Even under the baseline scenario of the Ageing Report, pension expenditure remains above 12% of GDP through 2070 (European Commission, 2024). This creates a persistent managerial challenge for public authorities: they must safeguard pension adequacy while preserving fiscal space for other priorities such as healthcare, education, and climate-related investment.

At the same time, Greece cannot assume that private pensions will automatically compensate for potential adequacy gaps. Evidence at the European Union level shows that the institutional environment for supplementary pensions remains fragmented and that cross-border products have not scaled effectively. The European Court of Auditors' assessment of the Pan-European Personal Pension Product (PEPP) illustrates limited uptake and weak provider incentives under the current design framework (European Court of Auditors, 2025; EIOPA, 2024). The limited uptake observed at EU level indicates that national policy levers – such as tax design, employer incentives, auto-enrolment mechanisms, and disclosure rules – are likely to be decisive if supplementary pensions are to expand in a way that supports retirement adequacy.

Private insurers could contribute by supplying funded savings products and lifetime income solutions, but their role depends on alignment between business strategies and public policy objectives. The managerial problem is therefore dual: public authorities must establish conditions that encourage long-term saving and fair-value retirement products, while insurers must design offerings that households understand and trust and that remain viable under longevity and market uncertainty. This dissertation addresses this problem by combining demographic and fiscal projections with evidence from pension economics and insurance research, focusing on how Greece can strengthen a multi-pillar pension approach without transferring excessive risk to individuals.

The study addresses this problem through stakeholder perceptions and exploratory empirical analysis rather than through direct forecasting of future pension outcomes.

1.4.2. Research Objectives

This dissertation has four objectives:

1. To analyse stakeholder perceptions of Greece's demographic ageing trajectory and its implications for PAYG sustainability and long-term fiscal space.

2. To examine how professionally relevant stakeholders perceive pension adequacy risks and potential retirement income gaps as population ageing progresses and pension reforms mature.
3. To evaluate which insurer capabilities and product mechanisms professionally relevant stakeholders consider most relevant for supporting supplementary retirement income provision in Greece.
4. To propose evidence-based recommendations for policymakers and insurance executives, grounded in stakeholder perspectives, that improve sustainability, participation, and consumer outcomes.

1.4.3. Research Questions

Main Research Question

How do professionally relevant stakeholders assess the implications of demographic change for the sustainability and adequacy of Greece's pension system, and under which conditions can supplementary funded solutions supported by private insurers contribute to sustainable retirement income provision?

Minor Research Questions

RQ1: How do professionally relevant stakeholders assess the long-term sustainability constraints that demographic change is likely to place on Greece's pay-as-you-go pension system?

RQ2: How do professionally relevant stakeholders perceive current and emerging pension adequacy risks in Greece as population ageing progresses and earlier pension reforms mature?

RQ3: Which insurer capabilities and product mechanisms do professionally relevant stakeholders consider most relevant for supporting supplementary retirement income provision in Greece?

RQ4: Which policy and regulatory measures do professionally relevant stakeholders consider most important for expanding supplementary pensions while protecting consumers and maintaining trust?

1.5 Research Gap and Contribution

While the existing literature provides substantial insight into demographic ageing and the fiscal sustainability of public pension systems in Greece, three important gaps remain. From a Doctor of Business Administration perspective, and informed by the author's professional and national familiarity with the Greek institutional context, these gaps are especially relevant for understanding how feasible pension reform is in practice.

First, the strategic role of private insurers remains underexplored. Previous studies have mainly examined pension reform from a state-centred perspective, with emphasis on parametric adjustment, fiscal consolidation, and public governance. Much less attention has been given to how private insurers, as institutional investors, risk-pooling actors, and product providers, might be integrated into Greece's evolving multi-pillar pension structure. In much of the literature, private insurance is still treated as a marginal or voluntary add-on rather than as a potentially strategic element within a more coordinated retirement-income system.

Second, there is still limited research that brings demographic change, regulation, and market design together in a practical way. While demographic projections and pension expenditure trends are well documented, fewer studies explain how these pressures should be translated into concrete policy choices. In the Greek context, it remains insufficiently clear how regulation, tax incentives, consumer protection, and insurer capabilities need to be aligned if private pension provision is to grow in a sustainable and credible way.

Third, the literature gives relatively little attention to trust and behavioural factors in post-crisis Greece. Repeated pension reforms and prolonged economic instability seem to have weakened confidence in long-term financial commitments. However, there is still limited understanding of how this affects households' willingness to engage with private pension and annuity products, and of what kind of governance or communication measures may help to reduce these barriers.

This study addresses these gaps by examining the relationship between demographic pressure, public pension sustainability, and the possible role of private insurers in Greece. By taking a policy- and governance-oriented perspective, it aims to provide evidence-based insights that are relevant to both policymakers and decision-makers in the insurance sector.

A further gap in the literature concerns the difference between reform ideas in principle and reform feasibility in practice. Many studies identify demographic pressure, fiscal imbalance, or the possible benefits of diversification, but fewer examine whether such reform ideas can actually be implemented in a context marked by weak trust, institutional fragmentation, and uneven market development. In the Greek case, this is especially important because pension reform has taken place under repeated economic and political pressure. This means that the success of reform depends not only on the technical quality of policy measures, but also on whether they are seen as credible and realistic by the main actors involved.

There is also limited research that brings together public pension sustainability and private insurance within one applied framework. In much of the literature, these areas are discussed separately, even though in practice they are closely connected. This makes it more difficult to understand how supplementary pension provision might develop in a system that still remains strongly centred on the public pillar. The present study addresses this issue by examining the relationship between public pension pressure, adequacy concerns, and the possible complementary role of private insurers within one analytical structure.

The contribution of the present study is therefore not only to identify gaps in the existing literature, but also to address them in a way that is relevant to practice. From a policy perspective, the dissertation contributes to the debate on how Greece might move towards a more coherent and better governed multi-pillar pension model without treating private provision as a simple substitute for the state. From a managerial perspective, it also contributes to understanding the conditions under which private insurers may play a stronger role, especially in relation to trust, product design, and regulatory credibility. In this sense, the study aims to contribute not only to academic discussion, but also to more informed decision-making in the fields of pension reform and retirement provision.

The study therefore focuses on the practical conditions under which pension reform can be supported by supplementary private provision. For policymakers, the analysis shows how demographic ageing creates pressure between fiscal sustainability and pension adequacy. For regulators, it points to the importance of transparency, governance, consumer protection, and trust. For private insurers, it shows that retirement products can only play a stronger role if they are understandable, well regulated, and clearly positioned as complementary to the public pension system.

Beyond its empirical focus, this dissertation is conceptually anchored in an institutional political economy perspective on pension reform. Rather than treating pension sustainability as a purely fiscal or actuarial issue, the analysis understands pension systems as institutional arrangements shaped by trust, governance quality, and historically embedded policy commitments. In ageing pay-as-you-go systems such as Greece, reform trajectories are therefore constrained not only by demographic arithmetic but also by legitimacy considerations and public confidence. This framework allows the study to integrate demographic pressure, adequacy risks, and private market development within a single analytical lens centred on institutional credibility and risk-sharing structures.

Accordingly, the study is designed to generate stakeholder-informed and practice-oriented insight for pension policy and insurance decision-making in Greece.

1.6 Scope and Delimitations

This dissertation focuses on Greece and examines pensions through the lens of demographic change and the role of private insurers. The public pension system is treated as the foundation of retirement income provision, while supplementary funded solutions are analysed as complements rather than substitutes. The empirical horizon aligns with official European projection frameworks extending to 2070, reflecting both the long-term nature of demographic ageing and the extended duration of pension commitments (European Commission, 2024).

This dissertation does not examine a single insurance company as a firm-specific case study. Instead, private insurers are considered more broadly as institutional actors within supplementary pension provision, with reference to the wider European pension and insurance context where relevant.

The dissertation does not provide a full actuarial valuation of Greece's pension liabilities, nor does it produce precise forecasts of financial market returns. Instead, it triangulates official demographic and fiscal projections with recent research on PAYG sustainability, funded pensions, and annuity markets to identify realistic policy pathways and governance requirements.

The study also recognises distributional limits. Some households have limited capacity to save, implying that supplementary pensions cannot replace the public pillar. Accordingly, the analysis pays particular attention to participation barriers, financial literacy, trust, and governance choices related to fees and disclosure, as these factors shape whether supplementary pensions can expand beyond higher-income groups and contribute to sustainability in practice.

1.7 Structure of the Dissertation

Chapter 1 introduces the research topic, motivation, and overall approach, and sets out the background, importance, research context, problem statement, objectives, research questions, and scope of the study. Chapter 2 reviews the literature on demographic ageing, PAYG sustainability, multi-pillar pension design, private insurance development, behavioural and trust-related barriers, and the regulatory and governance conditions relevant to supplementary pension expansion. Chapter 3 explains the research methodology, including the survey design, sampling approach, data gathering process, instrument development, and ethical considerations. Chapter 4 presents the empirical findings and statistical analysis. Chapter 5 discusses the findings in relation to the research questions and the wider literature and develops the managerial and policy implications of the study, as well as presenting the conclusions, recommendations, limitations, and directions for future research. Chapter 6 extends the analysis beyond the Greek case by examining the implications of the findings for other ageing societies, with particular reference to Italy, Portugal, and Germany. This comparative perspective helps to assess the broader relevance of the Greek experience and identifies transferable lessons for pension systems facing similar demographic and fiscal pressures. Chapter 7 concludes the dissertation by synthesising the empirical findings, comparative insights, and policy implications, and by outlining the overall contribution of the study to applied pension policy and insurance-sector decision-making.

Chapter 2 LITERATURE REVIEW AND RESEARCH BACKGROUND

This chapter deepens the contextual foundations established in Chapter 1 by detailing the historical evolution of the Greek pension system, the demographic drivers of long-run pressure, the macroeconomic conditions that shape pension financing capacity, and the development of private insurance in Greece. Together, these elements explain why Greece faces persistent trade-offs between fiscal sustainability and pension adequacy and why supplementary funded solutions and private providers have gained policy relevance. The chapter, therefore, provides essential background for the subsequent literature review and the design of the empirical analysis.

Part A: Research Background (Sections 2.1–2.4)

Sections 2.1 through 2.4 establish the contextual foundation for the empirical analysis. They document the historical evolution of the Greek pension system, the demographic pressures that are reshaping its financial dynamics, the macroeconomic constraints that limit policy space, and the current state of private insurance market development in Greece. Together, these sections provide the factual and institutional background necessary to frame the analytical literature review that follows.

2.1 Historical Background

Greece's pension system developed as a predominantly public, pay-as-you-go (PAYG) model embedded in a broader post-war welfare-state logic that prioritised social insurance and redistribution. Over time, however, the institutional architecture became highly fragmented, as multiple occupation-based funds and special regimes adopted different eligibility rules, benefit formulas, and contribution arrangements. This fragmentation supported negotiated protections for particular groups but reduced transparency and weakened the contribution–benefit link, which limited long-run financial discipline and made comprehensive reform politically difficult. The result was a pension landscape that combined strong public dominance with complex governance and uneven benefit outcomes across occupational categories (Kangur et al., 2021).

Kangur et al. (2021) is drawn upon extensively in this chapter as a foundational source on Greek pension reform and merits methodological scrutiny. The study is an IMF Working Paper based on quantitative analysis of pension system data covering the reform period through approximately 2019. Its principal conclusions concern the fiscal consolidation achieved through parametric reforms and the structural vulnerability of the PAYG model to demographic change. These conclusions are robust for the specific period and reform measures analysed, but several scope conditions limit their direct applicability to the present study. First, the analysis focuses primarily on fiscal sustainability indicators rather than adequacy or distributional outcomes, which means the study is informative about cost containment but less so about retirement income sufficiency. Second, as an IMF institutional publication, the study reflects an analytical lens that prioritises fiscal and macroeconomic stability, which may underweight social and trust-related dimensions of reform. Third, the study predates the introduction of TEKA (2022) and the post-2022 policy environment, meaning it cannot account for the most recent structural shift toward funded auxiliary provision. Contesting perspectives exist: Chrysanthopoulou et al. (2023) and Konstantinidou and Koumarianos (2025) offer assessments that give greater weight to adequacy concerns and the distributional consequences of the reforms that Kangur et al. (2021) characterise primarily in fiscal terms. The present study uses Kangur et al. (2021) for its institutional and historical account of the reform trajectory, while acknowledging that its normative framing and temporal scope differ from the adequacy-focused questions that motivate the primary research.

In the pre-crisis period, the pension system's vulnerabilities deepened because Greece maintained relatively generous entitlements while the economy and labour market did not generate a sufficiently stable and broad contribution base. Policy design also permitted multiple early-retirement pathways, which reduced effective retirement ages and increased the number of benefit years financed by the system. Although these features reflected social-policy choices and labour-market realities, they increased fiscal exposure under PAYG financing and created structural sensitivity to demographic change. In practice, PAYG systems depend on a stable ratio between contributors and beneficiaries, so any sustained shift in population structure or employment rapidly increases funding pressure (Kangur et al., 2021; OECD, 2024).

The sovereign debt crisis that began in 2009 acted as a decisive turning point because it transformed pension reform from a long-term policy issue into an immediate fiscal requirement. The recession compressed wages and employment, weakened contribution inflows, and increased pressure on public budgets. Under international financial assistance programmes, Greece implemented successive reform waves aimed at restoring fiscal sustainability and improving administrative coherence. These reforms included nominal and structural cuts to pension benefit levels, changes to indexation, tighter eligibility and accrual rules, increases in statutory and effective retirement ages, and repeated consolidation of pension funds. OECD country notes explicitly document the presence of benefit cuts and related measures as central elements of reform packages (OECD, 2024a).

Reforms during the mid-2010s also sought to address governance and equity issues created by fragmentation. The IMF's detailed assessment highlights that reforms implemented through 2015–2017 unified benefit and contribution rules, removed distortions, and reduced fragmentation and costs. This period emphasised consolidation and rationalisation alongside expenditure control, reflecting the need to stabilise public finances while establishing a more coherent administrative structure. These measures improved short- to medium-term fiscal indicators, but they also intensified debates about pension adequacy, distributional fairness, and trust in the stability of long-run promises, especially when households experienced repeated policy adjustments and uncertainty about future entitlement rules (Kangur et al., 2021; Laliotis et al., 2023).

An important implication of the crisis era is that pension reform in Greece did not occur as a single, discrete event; instead, it emerged as a cumulative process shaped by fiscal stress, external conditionality, and evolving domestic politics. This "reform sequencing" matters for behaviour and credibility. When citizens observe frequent changes to eligibility and benefit rules, they may rationally treat pension entitlements as less predictable, which can weaken long-term retirement planning and influence attitudes toward supplementary saving. Empirical work examining household behaviour during periods of institutional and economic turbulence in Greece shows how retirement and consumption decisions took place under uncertainty amid a series of reforms (Laliotis et al., 2023).

Greece did achieve considerable fiscal consolidation, but the longer-term sustainability issue did not go away. Demographic ageing kept putting pressure on PAYG financing. The European Commission's Ageing Report country fiche gives a long-run view of Greece's pension outlook under unchanged policy up to 2070. It shows that pensions are still expected to remain a major part of age-related public spending and that demographic change continues to matter for fiscal developments even after major reforms (European Commission, 2024). The IMF's 2025 consultation material makes a similar point. It notes that earlier reforms are expected to mature over time and may reduce pension expenditure relative to GDP in the long run. But this also means that reform effects take time and still depend on the wider macroeconomic and demographic setting (International Monetary Fund, 2025).

In response to this, Greece has gradually shown more interest in multi-pillar approaches alongside PAYG consolidation. The main step in this direction has been TEKA. Through TEKA, funded elements were strengthened within the auxiliary second pillar, and a funded defined-contribution (DC) structure was introduced for new labour-market entrants from 1 January 2022. OECD documentation describes TEKA as a funded DC system aimed at new entrants and some younger workers. This points to a policy move towards more diversified retirement income and less direct exposure to the demographic risks of a pure PAYG model (OECD, 2024). Research on occupational and supplementary pensions in Greece also treats TEKA as an important institutional change that may expand funded provision over time. At the same time, it raises practical questions about governance capacity, transition financing, and how broad participation can really become in an economy where saving capacity is uneven (Chrysanthopoulou et al., 2023).

Table 2.1: Evolution of the Greek Pension System and Reform Phases

Period	**System characteristics**	**Key policy features**
Pre-2009 (pre-crisis)	Fragmented PAYG system with strong public dominance	Multiple occupation-based funds; generous replacement rates; early retirement pathways; weak contribution–benefit link
2009–2014 (crisis onset)	Emergency fiscal adjustment phase	Pension benefit cuts, freezes, and indexation changes; increased retirement ages; eligibility tightening under adjustment programmes
2015–2017 (structural reform)	System consolidation and harmonisation	Unification of funds; standardised rules; contribution and benefit recalibration; governance simplification
Post-2018 (post-programme)	Consolidated PAYG with emerging funded elements	Continued parametric fine-tuning; focus on sustainability

Period	System characteristics	Key policy features
		indicators; gradual stabilisation
From 2022 onward	Multi-pillar orientation	Introduction of the TEKA-funded DC auxiliary pillar for new entrants

Overall, the historical evolution of Greece's pension system can be summarised as a movement from a fragmented, publicly dominated PAYG model toward a more consolidated and rules-harmonised structure, with an emerging strategy of partial diversification through funded auxiliary arrangements. The crisis period forced parametric adjustment and administrative consolidation, improving near-term fiscal control but raising social concerns about adequacy and stability. More recent developments—especially TEKA—reflect an attempt to embed funded mechanisms within the broader statutory framework, rather than relying solely on private voluntary markets. This trajectory directly aligns with Chapter 1's framing: Greece's pension debate now centres not only on controlling PAYG costs, but also on designing credible, well-governed complementary pillars that can share demographic and longevity risks without shifting excessive uncertainty onto households.

2.2 Demographic Background

Demographic change is one of the most persistent structural pressures on pension sustainability in Greece and directly strengthens the context set out in Chapter 1. Greece has combined very low fertility with rising life expectancy and a gradual decline in working-age cohorts over time, and this has shifted the population structure towards older age groups. For pensions, this is important because a predominantly pay-as-you-go (PAYG) system depends on a reasonably stable balance between contributors and beneficiaries. When the working-age population becomes smaller and the number of pensioners rises, the system has to respond in some way, whether through higher contributions, later retirement, lower benefits, or larger transfers from the state (European Commission, 2024).

One clear way of seeing this ageing pressure is through the old-age dependency ratio (OADR). The World Bank (2025) defines the OADR as the population aged 65 and over relative to the working-age population aged 15 to 64, expressed per 100 working-age individuals. Recent World Bank data show that Greece's old-age dependency ratio reached around 38% in 2024, meaning about 38 older persons for every 100 people of working age, and the ratio has been rising for decades. Eurostat projections point in the same direction and suggest that this pressure will become even stronger. According to Eurostat (2023), Greece's OADR is expected to rise above 60% by 2050, which would mean fewer than two working-age individuals for each older person and, in turn, greater pressure on PAYG financing.

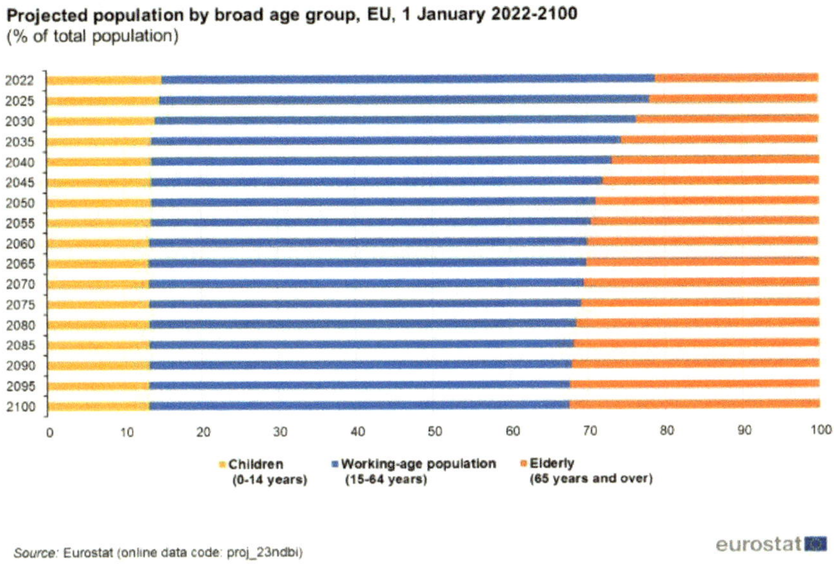

Figure 2.1 Projected Population by Age Group. Source: Eurostat (2023)

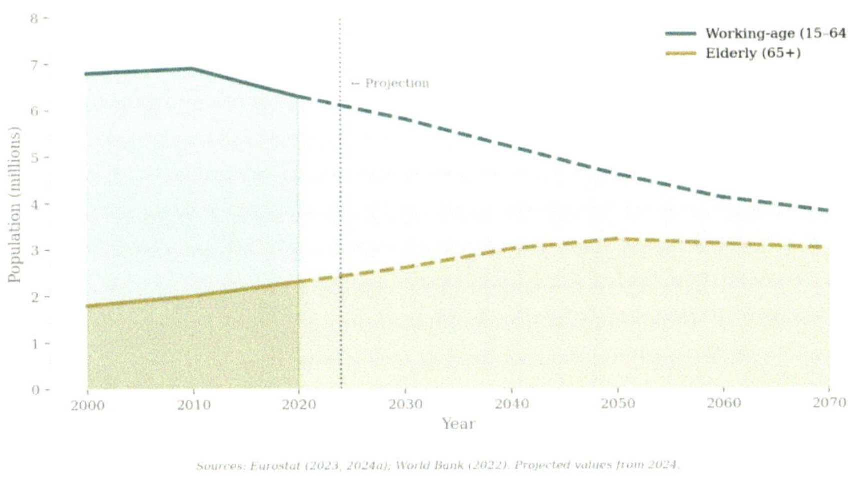

Figure 2.2 Projected population by age group, Greece, 2000–2070. Source: Eurostat (2023, 2024a)

Fertility trends deepen this structural challenge. At the EU level, Eurostat (2025a) reports a total fertility rate (TFR) of 1.38 births per woman in 2023, well below the replacement level of about 2.1. Greece remains among the countries experiencing sustained low fertility over long periods, which reduces the future working-age base and amplifies pension sustainability risks. Low fertility also tends to coincide with later family formation and labour-market uncertainty, which can reduce lifetime contributions and increase the likelihood of fragmented careers. These dynamics matter because contribution histories strongly shape pension adequacy under modern reformed rules that tighten the contribution–benefit link.

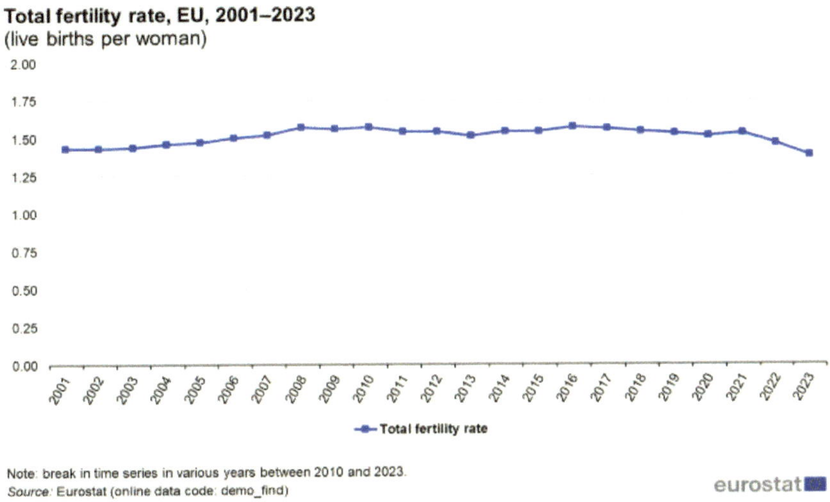

Figure 2.3 EU Fertility Rate (2001-2023). Source: Eurostat (2025a)

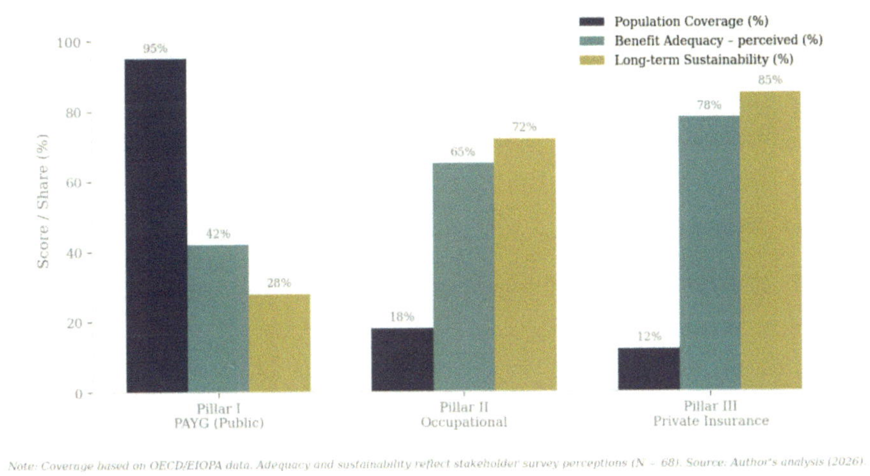

Figure 2.4 Multi-pillar pension framework, Greece. Source: Author’s analysis (2026)

Longevity further strengthens ageing pressure. Eurostat-based reporting places Greece’s life expectancy at birth at about 81.6 years in 2023, which increases expected years spent in retirement and therefore raises the importance of sustainable decumulation and longevity-risk management (Eurostat, 2024). Longer retirement periods increase the probability that households outlive assets, especially where individuals experience interrupted careers, periods of unemployment, or informal employment. From a pension-system perspective, longer lifespans raise the cost of delivering promised benefits unless retirement ages rise or benefit formulas adjust accordingly.

Ageing is visible in the overall population structure as well. Eurostat's (2024a) Demography reporting shows that Greece belongs to the oldest group of EU countries by median age, reporting 46.5 years in 2023, and Eurostat's population-structure updates highlight that ageing has been among the most pronounced in Greece over the last decade. This macro trend also produces geographic unevenness: Eurostat regional statistics show that several countries, including Greece, have regions with very high old-age dependency ratios, signalling that ageing pressure can concentrate locally and affect service capacity, labour markets, and fiscal demands at sub-national levels.

Regional differences also matter, as recent research shows that low fertility, rising life expectancy, and changing migration patterns do not affect all parts of Greece in the same way (Kalogeropoulos et al., 2024).

Overall, Greece's demographic outlook supports the core premise from Chapter 1: pension reform is not a one-off event but an ongoing necessity in an ageing society. The combination of high and rising OADR, low fertility, and longer life expectancy implies continuing pressure on PAYG financing and ongoing debates over adequacy, retirement ages, and the complementary role of funded pillars. This demographic background also strengthens the managerial and policy relevance of supplementary mechanisms, such as funded auxiliary provision and private-sector retirement products, provided that governance, affordability, and trust constraints do not limit participation to higher-income groups.

2.3 Economic Background

Greece's economic background shapes pension sustainability through four main channels: the size and stability of the contribution base, the state's fiscal capacity to support pensions, the effect of macroeconomic growth on debt dynamics, and the purchasing power and saving capacity of households. This section builds on Chapter 1 by showing why the post-2009 reform period improved short- to medium-term fiscal control but did not remove deeper constraints linked to economic structure and distributional pressure.

The sovereign debt crisis led to a long period of economic contraction, which reduced employment and wages and therefore weakened social security contribution revenues at a time when pension expenditure remained high. Although Greece has shown a strong recovery since the pandemic, this recovery still takes place in a broader crisis legacy marked by high public debt, sensitivity to macroeconomic shocks, and continuing structural reform needs. The IMF's (2025) Article IV materials describe Greece's near-term outlook as relatively favourable and project real GDP growth of around 2.1% in 2025, supported mainly by investment, including EU-funded projects, as well as by employment and income growth. At the same time, the IMF also warns against excessive increases in public wage and pension spending, which underlines the continuing importance of fiscal discipline for debt reduction and policy credibility.

Fiscal space remains one of the main macroeconomic constraints in this area. Eurostat (2025b) reports that Greece's government debt-to-GDP ratio reached 154.2% at the end of 2024, the highest in the European Union. Although the European Commission expects debt to decline over the medium term, the starting level remains very high. This means that pension policy continues to involve trade-offs between adequacy, healthcare, and wider investment priorities. The Greek Ministry of Finance reports 2.3% year-on-year growth in 2024, matching the pace recorded in 2023, which helps debt dynamics through the denominator effect and supports budget performance (Hellenic Ministry of National Economy and Finance, 2025). These macroeconomic improvements help explain why some short-run sustainability indicators improved after reform. However, they do not remove the longer-term pressure created by ageing and weaker workforce growth.

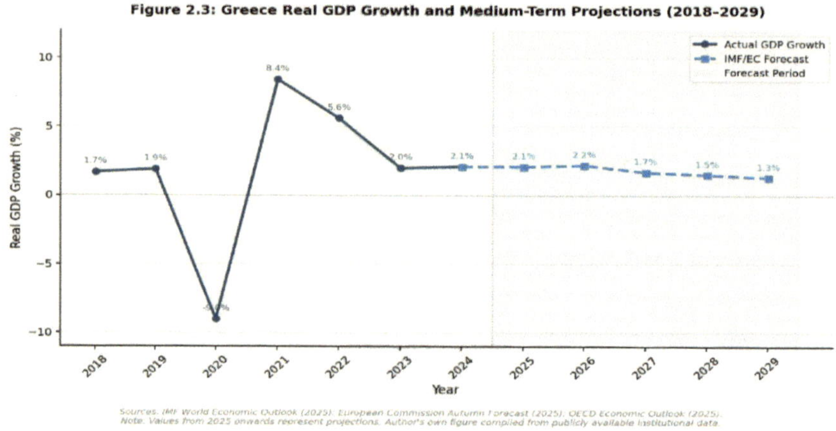

Figure 2.5 Greece Real GDP Growth and Projections (2018–2029)

Investment conditions also matter because they influence productivity and long-run wage growth, which in turn affect contribution revenue. Recent research points in the same direction. Makantasi and Valentis (2024), for example, discuss Greece's current economic challenges and stress the role of both internal and external factors in shaping growth capacity. Related IMF research on Greece's Recovery and Resilience Plan (RRP) argues that the plan can improve external balances and debt dynamics through stronger public saving and investment, but also makes clear that it is not sufficient on its own and still depends on prudent domestic policy choices (Aligishiev & Blotevogel, 2025). From a pension perspective, stronger investment-led growth can improve financing capacity, but it does not by itself resolve adequacy concerns or distributional tensions.

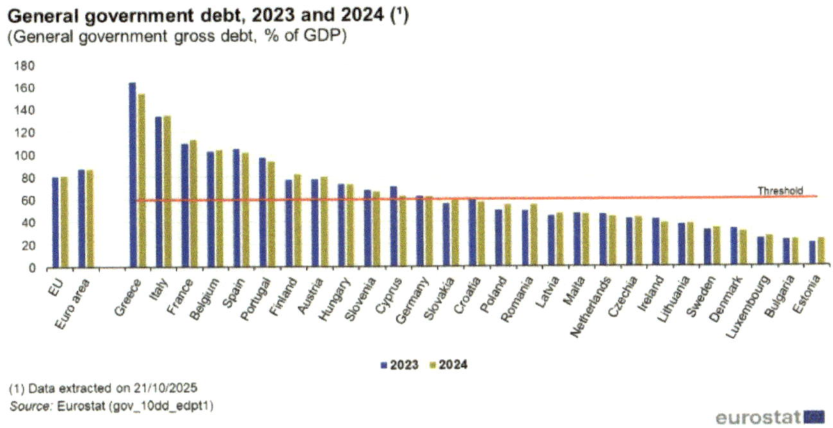

Figure 2.6 Debt-to-GDP ratio in the EU (2024). Source: Eurostat (2025b)

Distributional pressure also matters for retirement security. Research on inequality during and after the crisis shows that Greece experienced major welfare losses during the contraction and that inequality changed over the period 2004–2021 in ways closely linked to the crisis years (Danchev et al., 2024). This is also relevant for household saving behaviour. If disposable income remains under pressure, participation in supplementary pensions and private retirement products is likely to stay limited, especially among households outside higher-income groups.

Table 2.2: Key Macroeconomic Indicators for Pension Sustainability

Indicator	Latest value	Year	Relevance to pension sustainability
Real GDP growth	2.3%	2024	Supports employment, wage growth, and social security contribution revenues (Hellenic Ministry of National Economy and Finance, 2025)
Real GDP growth (projection)	2.1%	2025	Indicates near-term fiscal capacity to finance pensions (IMF, 2025)
Government debt-to-GDP ratio	154.2%	2024	Limits fiscal space for pension expenditure and indexation (Eurostat, 2025b)
HICP inflation (annual average)	3.0%	2024	Affects pension purchasing power and indexation pressures (ELSTAT, 2024)

2.4 Private Insurance Development in Greece

Private insurance has traditionally played a supplementary role in Greece's retirement system, since households have relied mainly on statutory public pensions for old-age income. Over the last decade, however, Greece's post-crisis reform path and the gradual move towards a more multi-pillar structure have made private insurers and related retirement products more relevant. Because the pension challenge is structural, shaped by ageing and fiscal limits, it also increases interest in complementary mechanisms that can diversify retirement income and help manage longevity risk (European Commission, 2024).

One reason for this growing relevance is the gradual recovery of market capacity and demand after the crisis. Market data point to continued premium growth. The Hellenic Association of Insurance Companies (2024) reports that the Greek insurance market recorded premium increases in 2023, with life insurance continuing to grow. More recent supervisory data from the Bank of Greece (2025a) show that total assets of insurance corporations reached €21.5 billion in the second quarter of 2025. This indicates a sizeable balance-sheet base and underlines the role of insurers as institutional investors. For pensions, this matters because a stronger and more stable insurance sector can support long-term savings products, including life insurance, unit-linked products, and annuities, and can therefore provide part of the infrastructure for supplementary retirement provision. However, when placed in a comparative European context, Greece's private pension market remains underdeveloped relative to its EU peers. EIOPA's (2024) pan-European data indicate that insurance penetration in Greece, measured as total insurance premiums as a percentage of GDP, stands at approximately 2.1%, compared to an EU average of around 7.5% and figures above 10% in more mature markets such as the Netherlands and Denmark. Pension-specific assets under management in Greece represent a substantially smaller share of GDP than the EU average, reflecting the structural dominance of the public PAYG pillar and the limited development of the second and third pillars to date. This gap underscores both the challenge and the opportunity: the conditions that have constrained private pension growth also define the policy space in which targeted reforms could yield meaningful results.

Research also helps explain what drives life insurance demand in Greece. A recent empirical study using Greek quarterly data from 2007 to 2021 examines the macroeconomic determinants of life insurance demand and shows that income conditions and wider macroeconomic stability influence households' willingness to purchase long-term protection and savings products (Stathopoulos & Vrontos, 2025). Although the study deals with life insurance rather than pensions directly, it still points to an important issue for retirement policy: broader participation in long-term financial products depends heavily on economic confidence and reasonably stable disposable income.

At the same time, supplementary retirement provision in Greece has also developed through occupational and other funded arrangements that can interact with private-sector capacity. Research on occupational pension funds in Greece shows that this pillar is still small compared with the dominant pay-as-you-go system, but it is becoming more relevant in terms of diversification and efficiency, especially as reforms encourage funded accumulation and improvements in governance (Chrysanthopoulou et al., 2023). This fits the broader direction of reform in Greece, where the aim is not to rely only on PAYG financing but gradually to strengthen funded elements as well. That can increase demand for professional asset management and retirement-income solutions, which are areas where insurers may contribute through product design, risk pooling, and long-term investment management.

Regulation and trust also matter for the development of private insurance. Greek insurers operate within the EU's Solvency II framework, which places emphasis on risk-based capital, governance, and disclosure. At EU level, EIOPA's monitoring and stress-testing frameworks provide a broader basis for assessing insurers' resilience under adverse conditions (EIOPA, 2025). At national level, the Bank of Greece reports that the Greek insurance market remained adequately capitalised in 2024 despite wider macroeconomic and geopolitical pressures, which supports the credibility needed for long-term retirement products.

Even so, several limits remain important for this dissertation. First, participation is likely to remain uneven because voluntary retirement saving depends on stable employment and income, and these were weakened for many households during the crisis and in the years that followed. Second, trust remains fragile. Repeated pension reforms and crisis-era welfare adjustments may reduce confidence in long-term promises, and this can also affect how private retirement products are perceived unless transparency and consumer protection remain strong. Third, market growth on its own does not automatically produce inclusive retirement outcomes. Without well-designed defaults, fair pricing, and clear disclosure, supplementary provision may remain concentrated among higher-income groups. From a policy and governance point of view, this raises the broader question of how private insurers can be integrated into the pension system without weakening social adequacy or public trust.

Overall, private insurance in Greece has grown in market scale and institutional capacity and has become more relevant in a reform environment that increasingly supports funded accumulation and multi-pillar solutions. However, private insurers can support pension sustainability only if policy and regulation protect consumers, maintain trust, and ensure that supplementary products complement rather than substitute adequate public provision for households with limited saving capacity (European Commission, 2024).

The discussion so far also shows that private insurance in Greece cannot be assessed in isolation from the wider structure of pension provision. To understand whether private insurers can contribute meaningfully to pension sustainability, it is necessary to consider the broader logic of multi-pillar pension systems, the behavioural and trust-related conditions that shape participation, and the regulatory and governance frameworks that determine whether supplementary pension provision can expand in a credible and socially legitimate way.

2.4.1 Limitations of Private Pension Provision

Private pension provision also has limits. It can support the Greek pension system, but it cannot replace the public pension pillar. This is especially important for households with low or unstable income, since many people may not be able to save regularly for retirement.

There is also the issue of complexity. Pension and insurance products often include fees, investment risk, long time horizons, and conditions that are not always easy to understand. If these points are not explained clearly, trust may remain low and consumers may choose products that do not fully meet their needs.

Another concern is that voluntary private pensions may mainly attract higher-income households and people with stable employment. This would limit their contribution to the wider pension system and could increase differences in retirement outcomes.

Part B: Analytical Literature Review (Sections 2.5–2.9)

Sections 2.5 through 2.9 shift from contextual background to analytical engagement with the scholarly and policy literature. They examine theoretical frameworks and empirical findings relevant to multi-pillar pension design, behavioural and trust-related barriers to supplementary pension participation, and the regulatory and governance conditions under which private provision can expand effectively. These sections directly inform the research questions and the interpretive framework applied in Chapters 4 and 5.

2.5 Multi-pillar pension systems and the logic of diversification

Multi-pillar pension systems are widely discussed in the literature as a response to the structural limits of purely pay-as-you-go pension provision in ageing societies. Their basic logic is diversification. Instead of relying on a single institutional mechanism to provide retirement income, multi-pillar systems seek to combine public redistribution, funded savings, and in some cases voluntary private provision in a way that spreads risk more broadly across the state, employers, financial institutions, and households.

The original policy rationale behind multi-pillar pension design is that different pension pillars perform different functions. Public pensions are generally expected to protect against poverty in old age and to provide a socially legitimate minimum level of retirement income. Funded occupational and private pensions, by contrast, are usually seen as supplementary. They are expected to smooth consumption over the life course and reduce exclusive dependence on intergenerational transfers. In this sense, a multi-pillar system is not just an institutional arrangement, but also a framework for distributing different forms of risk. Demographic risk, fiscal risk, labour-market risk, inflation risk, and longevity risk are spread across several channels rather than concentrated in one public scheme.

This logic is particularly relevant in the Greek case. As the previous sections have shown, Greece remains heavily dependent on a public pension system that is still largely shaped by pay-as-you-go financing, despite repeated reforms and the introduction of funded auxiliary elements. Such dependence creates vulnerability because demographic deterioration directly affects the balance between contributors and beneficiaries. In systems with stronger funded pillars, part of retirement income depends not only on the contributions of the active population but also on capital accumulation, investment returns, and long-term asset management. This does not remove risk, but it changes its composition. A funded pillar is less directly exposed to short-term demographic shocks, even though it becomes more exposed to market volatility and governance quality.

At the same time, the literature does not treat multi-pillar systems as universally superior in all contexts. Their effectiveness depends on institutional design, sequencing, and the broader socio-economic environment in which they operate. In countries with high financial literacy, stable employment paths, strong regulatory oversight, and developed capital markets, supplementary funded pensions may work as a relatively effective complement to public provision. In settings marked by distrust, fragmented work histories, weak enforcement, or limited saving capacity, however, the expansion of funded pensions may remain shallow or may produce unequal outcomes. This is why the literature increasingly treats pension diversification not simply as a technical reform model, but as a governance issue.

An important issue in this debate is the difference between diversification in theory and inclusiveness in practice. A pension system may formally contain several pillars without producing broad-based diversification in actual retirement outcomes. If participation in supplementary pensions is concentrated among higher-income households or workers in particular formal sectors, the existence of private or occupational pillars does not necessarily strengthen resilience across society as a whole. Instead, it may create a divided structure, in which one group has access to diversified retirement income while another remains largely dependent on a public system that is already under pressure. This is especially relevant in Greece, where uneven labour-market attachment and limited household saving capacity may restrict the wider reach of funded solutions.

From a policy perspective, multi-pillar models also raise the question of complementarity versus substitution. The literature generally suggests that supplementary pensions are more effective when they complement rather than replace public pension provision. If private solutions are presented as substitutes for a weakened public pension system, they are more likely to face political resistance and lower levels of public trust, particularly in post-crisis settings.

This distinction is especially important in Greece. The political and social legacy of repeated pension reforms means that any perception of public retrenchment in favour of private marketisation may be met with scepticism. For this reason, the strategic relevance of private insurers does not depend only on their ability to offer pension products, but also on whether these products can be embedded in an institutional framework that is seen as fair, understandable, and supportive of retirement security. In other words, the success of multi-pillar reform depends not only on product availability, but also on political legitimacy and institutional credibility.

A further point in the literature is that diversification should be understood in dynamic rather than static terms. Pension systems evolve over time, and the interaction between pillars also changes. In the Greek case, the introduction of TEKA shows how funded components may first emerge in one limited part of the system and only later shape broader retirement provision. This means that the transition towards a more genuinely multi-pillar structure is likely to be gradual rather than immediate. Such gradualism has advantages, because it allows institutional learning and regulatory adjustment, but it also creates transition challenges, including questions of coverage, intergenerational fairness, and the overlap between legacy PAYG obligations and new funded accumulations.

For this reason, the literature increasingly argues that the value of a multi-pillar system should not be judged only by its formal architecture, but by how effectively the pillars interact. A fragmented coexistence of public, occupational, and private arrangements is not enough. What matters is whether these pillars together produce retirement outcomes that are sustainable, adequate, and socially legitimate. This broader understanding of diversification is especially relevant for the present dissertation, because it places the role of private insurers within a system-level framework rather than treating them as isolated market actors.

Much of the literature therefore suggests that multi-pillar pension systems are best understood as institutional attempts to diversify risk, broaden retirement income sources, and reduce systemic dependence on any single financing mechanism. However, their practical value depends on governance, trust, participation, and the extent to which funded pillars are integrated into a socially legitimate pension model. For Greece, this means that the central issue is not simply whether funded provision should be strengthened, but how this can be done in a way that remains compatible with public trust, regulatory capacity, and the continuing importance of the public pension pillar.

At the same time, the institutional logic of diversification does not automatically lead to broad-based participation in supplementary pension arrangements. Even where multi-pillar systems appear conceptually attractive, their practical success depends on whether households are willing and able to engage with long-term retirement products. This makes behavioural and trust-related barriers a central part of the analysis.

A further distinction in the literature concerns diversification at the system level and diversification at the household level. These two ideas are related, but they are not the same. At the system level, diversification refers to the coexistence of different pension pillars with different financing logics, such as tax-financed redistributive benefits, contribution-based public pensions, occupational funds, and private savings vehicles. At the household level, however, diversification refers to whether individuals and families actually receive retirement income from more than one source. A country may therefore appear institutionally diversified while large parts of the population remain dependent in practice on a single public pension stream. This matters because the resilience of a pension system cannot be judged only by legal design or formal structure, but also by how widely diversified retirement income is across the population.

This issue is particularly relevant in Greece. Even where supplementary pension arrangements exist in legal or institutional form, their practical reach may remain narrow if participation is concentrated among higher-income groups, workers in more stable employment, or individuals with stronger financial capability. In such a setting, the existence of supplementary pillars does not automatically reduce aggregate vulnerability. Instead, it may create a segmented retirement landscape.

2.6 Behavioural and trust barriers to supplementary pension uptake

Although supplementary pension provision is often presented as a rational response to demographic ageing and fiscal pressure, actual participation in funded pension products depends not only on economic incentives but also on behavioural and psychological factors. In practice, households do not make retirement decisions under idealised conditions of perfect information, full confidence, and long-term planning discipline. Instead, participation in pension saving is shaped by bounded rationality, trust in institutions, perceived product complexity, and wider experiences of economic stability or instability.

A recurring theme in the pension literature is that long-term saving decisions are unusually vulnerable to behavioural frictions. Retirement planning requires individuals to assess uncertain future income needs, long time horizons, inflation, longevity risk, and investment uncertainty. These are difficult decisions even in stable institutional environments. As a result, many individuals postpone action, rely on default options, or avoid engagement altogether when products seem too complex or abstract. This helps explain why supplementary pension uptake is often lower than policy designers expect, even where the long-term need for additional retirement saving is clear.

In Greece, these behavioural barriers are likely to be intensified by the legacy of the sovereign debt crisis and repeated pension reforms. Households that have experienced benefit cuts, economic instability, unemployment, wage compression, or abrupt changes in institutional rules may be less willing to commit resources to long-duration financial products. In such settings, low participation cannot be explained solely by limited income. It may also reflect low institutional confidence. If people do not trust that rules will remain stable, that products are fairly designed, or that future benefits will materialise as expected, then even well-designed supplementary pension instruments may struggle to gain traction.

Trust, therefore, becomes a central variable in the transition toward stronger supplementary pension provision. Trust operates on at least three levels. First, there is trust in the state and in the broader pension reform process. Individuals must believe that the institutional framework within which private and occupational pensions operate will remain reasonably stable over time. Second, there is trust in providers, including insurers, pension managers, and intermediaries. Products may be formally sound, but if they are associated with opacity, aggressive selling, or unclear benefit structures, participation is likely to remain weak. Third, there is trust in one's own ability to make financially meaningful choices. Low confidence in financial understanding can itself discourage participation.

This third dimension is closely related to financial literacy. The literature frequently shows that participation in supplementary pensions is associated with the ability to understand risk, compounding, inflation, and retirement income trade-offs. However, financial literacy should not be interpreted too narrowly as an individual shortcoming. Product design and communication also matter. A well-governed supplementary pension market should not depend on high financial sophistication alone. If products are too difficult for ordinary households to understand, this is partly a governance failure rather than simply a consumer deficit.

Financial literacy is also important in this context. Lusardi and Mitchell (2014) describe it as the ability to understand and use basic financial concepts such as interest compounding, inflation, risk diversification, and long-term financial decision-making. Existing research shows that stronger financial literacy is generally associated with more active retirement planning and greater engagement with long-term financial products. At the same time, OECD evidence suggests that financial literacy remains limited across many countries, which helps explain why individuals often rely on inertia, default options, or avoid complex financial products altogether. In the Greek context, this issue is especially relevant. Repeated pension reforms and economic instability may have weakened not only trust, but also the perceived value of engaging in complex pension decisions. If households expect rules to change repeatedly, they may be less willing to invest time in understanding pension products in detail. In addition, EU survey evidence shows that financial literacy remains uneven across the Union, which reinforces the importance of product simplicity, standardised disclosure, and clear communication. This does not mean that individuals act irrationally. Rather, it suggests that supplementary pension products should be designed in a way that does not depend on high levels of financial sophistication. For this reason, measures such as plain-language communication, default enrolment mechanisms, and consumer protection become especially important alongside financial education efforts.

For this reason, simplicity and transparency are repeatedly highlighted in the literature as preconditions for wider supplementary pension uptake. Individuals are more likely to engage with retirement products when contribution mechanisms, fee structures, expected outcomes, and withdrawal conditions are communicated clearly. By contrast, complicated products may increase decision paralysis, suspicion, or withdrawal from the market altogether. This is especially relevant for insurers, whose strategic role in pension systems depends not just on product availability, but on their capacity to translate technical financial mechanisms into understandable and credible retirement solutions.

Behavioural factors also interact with labour-market structure. Individuals with irregular employment, unstable income, or fragmented contribution histories may perceive supplementary pensions as unrealistic or inaccessible. In such circumstances, even those who recognise the inadequacy of future public pensions may still not participate in voluntary retirement products. This helps explain why low uptake of supplementary pensions cannot be understood simply as a failure of awareness. It may also reflect broader insecurity about the affordability of long-term commitments. In this sense, behavioural barriers are deeply connected to structural economic conditions.

A further dimension relates to perceptions of fairness. Supplementary pensions gain acceptance when individuals perceive fair value, reasonable fees, and a balanced allocation of risk between providers and consumers.

The literature also suggests that behavioural barriers can be partly mitigated through institutional design. Policy tools such as auto-enrolment, simple default funds, standardised disclosure, and strong consumer protection can reduce the burden on individual decision-making. These measures do not eliminate behavioural frictions, but they can make participation less dependent on continuous active optimisation by individuals. For countries such as Greece, where trust and financial confidence may be fragile, such institutional supports may be more important than relying solely on voluntary market demand.

In the Greek context, therefore, the question is not simply whether supplementary pensions are economically desirable, but whether they are behaviourally and institutionally credible. A pension reform model that assumes rational and enthusiastic uptake of complex private products is unlikely to succeed. A more realistic approach is to recognise that confidence, trust, and product intelligibility are part of the pension sustainability problem itself. This insight is central to the present dissertation, because it links demographic and fiscal pressures to the practical conditions under which funded pension expansion may or may not be socially feasible.

Existing studies indicate that the expansion of supplementary pension provision is constrained not only by regulation and affordability, but also by behavioural and trust-related barriers. These include product complexity, low institutional confidence, limited financial literacy, insecure income conditions, and concerns about fairness. In Greece, such barriers are likely to be particularly salient given the post-crisis environment. This makes trust and governance not secondary issues, but core conditions for the viability of any stronger role for private insurers in retirement provision.

These behavioural and trust-related barriers are not shaped by individual attitudes alone. They are also influenced by the regulatory and governance environment within which pension products are designed, distributed, and supervised. For this reason, the analysis must now turn to the institutional conditions under which supplementary pension provision can expand in a credible and sustainable way.

2.7 Regulatory and governance conditions for supplementary pension

The expansion of supplementary pension provision depends not only on market demand or demographic necessity, but also on the regulatory and governance framework within which such provision operates. Pension markets are institutionally sensitive because they involve very long time horizons, uncertain outcomes, and a strong asymmetry of information between providers and consumers. For this reason, the literature consistently treats governance quality and regulatory credibility as central conditions for the success of funded pension arrangements.

In the Greek case, this issue is particularly important because supplementary pension provision remains relatively underdeveloped and public trust in long-term financial arrangements is still fragile. Under such conditions, regulatory credibility becomes part of the market itself. Households are more likely to engage with supplementary products when they believe that providers are adequately supervised, that product information is transparent, and that legal protections are meaningful in practice. Conversely, weak or unclear regulatory frameworks can undermine uptake even before product evaluation begins.

The literature suggests that regulatory design matters especially in four areas: prudential supervision, tax and incentive structures, enrolment architecture, and consumer protection. Prudential supervision concerns the financial resilience and governance quality of insurers and pension providers. This includes capital adequacy, asset-liability management, disclosure requirements, and operational governance. In the EU context, Solvency II provides a broad prudential framework for insurers, while supervisory institutions such as EIOPA contribute to harmonisation and cross-border regulatory coordination. These frameworks matter because they support long-term credibility. Retirement products ultimately depend on people's belief that providers will remain solvent and meet their obligations, even many years into the future.

Financial soundness alone, however, is not enough to encourage participation. Incentives are just as important. The literature makes this point repeatedly. The extent to which people participate in supplementary pensions depends heavily on tax rules, contribution incentives, and employer arrangements. Products and regulation may be sound, but if households and employers see little reason to participate, uptake will remain low. This is one reason why supplementary pension development varies so much across Europe, even where demographic pressures are similar. National policy choices influence whether funded provision remains marginal or becomes a more established part of retirement planning.

Greece is a clear example of this problem. Affordability remains tight, and private retirement saving has never expanded on a broad scale. In this context, tax incentives are more than a technical detail. They influence whether supplementary pensions are seen as a realistic option for the wider population or mainly as niche products for higher-income groups. The literature suggests that where incentive structures are weak, funded pension expansion may stagnate even when public debate strongly recognises future adequacy risks.

A third regulatory dimension concerns enrolment architecture. Many pension systems have found that voluntary participation alone often produces limited and unequal take-up. As a result, policy tools such as auto-enrolment, default investment pathways, and simplified onboarding procedures have received growing attention in the comparative literature. These measures matter because they reduce the behavioural burden placed on individuals. Rather than assuming active and fully informed retirement planning by all households, they create structured default mechanisms that encourage broader participation while preserving some degree of choice.

For Greece, such mechanisms may be particularly relevant because the challenge is not only to create pension products, but also to normalise supplementary pension participation in a context where the long-term saving culture may remain relatively weak. Auto-enrolment and similar measures can help address participation inertia, but they also raise governance questions. If default mechanisms are used, transparency, fairness, fee control, and opt-out rights become even more important. This is why enrolment architecture and consumer protection are closely linked.

Consumer protection is the fourth major dimension. The literature shows that funded pension markets cannot be considered successful merely because participation expands. The quality of products and the fairness of outcomes matter equally. Consumers need to be protected against opaque fee structures, unrealistic return expectations, inappropriate risk transfer, and product complexity that obscures long-term value. Standardised disclosure, suitability rules, plain-language communication, and effective complaints mechanisms all play a role in sustaining confidence. In retirement products, where outcomes may become visible only many years later, weak consumer protection can have particularly damaging consequences.

This is where the role of private insurers becomes analytically important. Insurers are not merely passive actors responding to regulation; they are also strategic participants whose product design choices influence how supplementary pension systems evolve. If insurers emphasise clarity, transparency, and protection against longevity risk, they can strengthen the social legitimacy of supplementary pension provision. If, by contrast, products are perceived as overly complex, expensive, or insufficiently aligned with consumer needs, regulatory support alone may not be enough to generate trust.

The literature also raises the question of coordination between national and European frameworks. EU-level initiatives such as the Pan-European Personal Pension Product were intended, at least in part, to reduce fragmentation and support a more integrated supplementary pension market. Yet the evidence so far suggests that implementation has been limited and uneven. This indicates that cross-border pension solutions cannot succeed purely through formal regulatory creation; they also require national tax compatibility, provider incentives, and consumer acceptance. For Greece, this means that European frameworks may support reform, but they cannot replace domestic governance choices.

Literature Search Strategy

The literature review was conducted through a systematic search of academic databases including Google Scholar, JSTOR, ScienceDirect, and the OECD iLibrary, supplemented by policy repositories of the World Bank, IMF, European Commission, and EIOPA. The primary search terms included "Greek pension system", "pension sustainability Greece", "demographic ageing pension reform", "private insurers supplementary pension", "multi-pillar pension system", "pension adequacy Southern Europe", "behavioural barriers pension saving", and "pension governance transparency". These terms were used individually and in combination, with the search focused primarily on publications from 2015 onwards in order to capture the post-crisis reform environment, while retaining foundational references from earlier periods where necessary for theoretical grounding. Studies were included on the basis of relevance to the Greek institutional context, conceptual contribution to the multi-pillar literature, or empirical evidence on pension behaviour, insurer roles, or regulatory design. Sources that were purely theoretical without applied relevance, or that addressed pension systems with no meaningful comparability to the Greek case, were excluded. This approach is consistent with the applied orientation of the dissertation, which prioritises analytically relevant and institutionally grounded evidence over exhaustive bibliographic coverage.

The initial database searches returned a large volume of results, which were screened in two stages. In the first stage, titles and abstracts were reviewed for relevance to pension sustainability, demographic ageing, private insurance, and the Greek or Southern European context. Studies meeting at least one of these criteria were retained for full-text review. In the second stage, full texts were assessed for methodological rigour, recency, and direct applicability to the research questions. Empirical studies that relied solely on single-country data from non-comparable institutional contexts, or policy documents that pre-dated the post-2010 reform period without conceptual relevance, were excluded. The final selection comprised peer-reviewed journal articles, IMF and World Bank working papers, OECD and EIOPA publications, and selected institutional reports that met the relevance and quality thresholds described above. Where studies presented contesting findings or methodological limitations relevant to the research questions, these are noted explicitly in the review sections that follow.

2.8 Interim Synthesis of the Literature

The literature reviewed in this chapter presents the Greek pension challenge as a multi-dimensional problem shaped by demographic ageing, fiscal constraints, institutional legacy, market development, behavioural barriers, and regulatory design. The evidence suggests that no single reform lever is likely to resolve these pressures in isolation. Instead, the long-term sustainability and adequacy of retirement provision in Greece depend on the interaction between public pension reform, the gradual development of funded supplementary mechanisms, and the governance conditions under which private insurers may contribute to retirement security.

Across the reviewed literature, the Greek pension system is consistently characterised by strong demographic pressures, constrained fiscal capacity, and repeated reform efforts that have yet to establish a coherent and sustainable multi-pillar framework.

A methodological note is warranted regarding the use of OECD publications throughout this review. OECD sources are used extensively because they provide the most comprehensive and comparable cross-national data on pension systems, demographic projections, and insurance market conditions. However, OECD publications function as authoritative reference material and carry an institutional perspective that reflects the policy positions of member-state governments. Their recommendations tend to favour funded mechanisms, individual responsibility, and market-based solutions, which reflects the broader normative orientation of the OECD's pension reform agenda. This does not invalidate the empirical content of OECD reports, but it does mean that findings and recommendations should be read as institutionally situated rather than as neutral evidence. Where OECD findings are used in this review, they are assessed for their specific empirical scope and the conditions under which their conclusions apply, rather than adopted wholesale as authoritative conclusions about what Greek pension reform should entail.

Table 2.3: Comparative Synthesis of Key Empirical Studies

Study	**Method**	**Principal Findings**	**Scope Limitations**
Kangur et al. (2021)	IMF quantitative analysis of Greek pension reform data to 2019	Reforms improved fiscal sustainability; PAYG structurally vulnerable to demographic change	Fiscal focus; pre-dates TEKA (2022); limited coverage of adequacy and distributional outcomes
Chrysanthopoulou et al. (2023)	Efficiency analysis of Greek occupational pension funds	Variable fund efficiency; governance quality affects outcomes significantly	Limited to occupational funds; does not address retail private insurance market
Nektarios & Tinios (2019)	World Bank policy analysis of NDC reform attempts	Repeated NDC reform attempts obstructed by political economy constraints	Pre-dates 2019 reform consolidation; limited coverage of supplementary pension developments
Konstantinidou & Koumarianos (2025)	Policy analysis of flexible retirement pathways in Greece	Flexible pathways may improve adequacy but create fiscal risks; governance conditions decisive	Focus on public system flexibility; limited discussion of private supplementary provision
OECD (2024a)	Cross-national comparative analysis; OECD Pensions Outlook	Multi-pillar diversification reduces demographic risk; funded components improve sustainability	Institutional perspective favouring market mechanisms; conclusions not always transferable to low-trust contexts

Study	Method	Principal Findings	Scope Limitations
Rotschedl et al. (2024)	Comparative quantitative analysis of PAYG sustainability 1993-2023	PAYG systems address short-term imbalances but remain highly exposed to long-term demographic mismatches	Comparative design limits country-specific conclusions; does not address supplementary provision

While multi-pillar pension models are frequently advocated in the literature, their effectiveness appears to be highly context-dependent, particularly with regard to labour market structures and institutional capacity.

These findings underscore the need for a more integrated analysis of how private insurance mechanisms may complement public pension provision within Greece's specific institutional and regulatory environment, thereby informing the analytical focus of the subsequent chapters.

These considerations provide the analytical foundation for the subsequent examination of governance mechanisms and policy options in the following chapters.

At the same time, the literature shows that the Greek pension challenge cannot be explained only by demographic pressure or fiscal constraints. These factors are clearly important, but they are closely connected with issues such as trust, institutional credibility, and the practical design of supplementary provision. This is important because it shows that pension sustainability in Greece is not only a financial issue. It is also a governance issue, because the success of reform depends on whether public and private actors operate within a framework that is seen as coherent, fair, and credible over time.

Another important point in the literature is that the role of private insurers should not be examined separately from the wider pension system. Their relevance depends not only on their technical ability to provide funded savings products or longevity-risk solutions, but also on how these products fit into the broader pension structure. If private provision is seen as a substitute for a weaker public pillar, it is likely to face more resistance. If it is developed as a complement to public provision, supported by clear regulation and consumer protection, it may be more acceptable both politically and socially. This makes the Greek case especially relevant, because the literature shows that multi-pillar reform is not only about financial diversification, but also about legitimacy and institutional design.

The review also makes clear that the expansion of supplementary pensions depends on more than the existence of products. Behavioural barriers, affordability constraints, fragmented employment histories, and weak trust in long-term commitments all affect whether households are likely to participate. This means that the debate on pension reform should not focus only on what pension products can be offered, but also on whether the conditions exist for broad and credible participation. In this sense, the literature reviewed in this chapter supports the need for a more applied analysis that links demographic pressure, regulatory design, insurer capability, and stakeholder perception within one framework.

The literature reviewed in this chapter shows that the Greek pension system faces pressure from several directions at the same time. Demographic ageing weakens the contribution base of the pay-as-you-go system, while fiscal constraints limit the ability of the state to respond only through higher public spending. At the same time, pension adequacy remains important, because reforms that improve sustainability may also reduce the level of future retirement income.

For this reason, the role of private insurers is examined in this dissertation as a complementary issue. Private insurers may contribute through supplementary pension products, long-term savings, annuities, and longevity-risk management. However, the literature also shows that this role depends on important conditions. These include regulation, transparency, consumer protection, product design, and public trust.

This means that the study does not treat private insurance as a direct solution to the pension problem. Instead, it examines whether private insurers can support a more balanced pension structure under the right institutional and regulatory conditions. This provides the basis for the empirical analysis in the following chapters.

2.9 Research Gaps and Implications for the Present Study

First, the literature reveals a clear strategic gap regarding the role of private insurers within the Greek pension system. Existing studies tend to treat private pensions either as a marginal, voluntary supplement or as an abstract component of idealised multi-pillar models. What is largely missing is a systematic analysis of how insurance companies, drawing on their core competencies in long-term investment, longevity risk pooling, and product development, could function as an integrated and strategic element of a coordinated retirement income system in Greece. In particular, the literature offers limited insight into the concrete contribution such actors could make under Greece's specific market conditions, characterised by limited scale, fragmented provision, and historically low levels of public trust.

Second, there is a notable disconnect between demographic and fiscal diagnosis on the one hand and regulatory and product-level design on the other. While the long-term implications of population ageing and fiscal constraints are well established, relatively few studies translate these macro-level challenges into coherent frameworks that link demographic pressures to concrete regulatory, tax, and product design choices. As a result, the literature often falls short of explaining how regulation, incentive structures, consumer protection, and insurer business models must be aligned to enable the sustainable expansion of private pension provision without compromising adequacy or system stability.

Third, the literature insufficiently addresses the role of trust and household behaviour in the Greek context. Although confidence and participation are widely recognised as important factors in pension systems, existing research rarely engages with the specific effects of repeated pension reforms, economic instability, and policy reversals on risk perception and long-term saving behaviour among Greek households. The implications of this trust deficit for governance arrangements, communication strategies, and the demand for long-term pension and annuity products remain under-researched.

A further gap in the literature concerns the relationship between formal pension design and practical acceptance. Many studies discuss multi-pillar pension systems in institutional or economic terms, but fewer examine whether such arrangements are actually seen as legitimate and credible by the actors expected to operate within them. In the Greek case, this is especially important because the expansion of supplementary pensions is not only a matter of technical design, but also of whether such arrangements can gain acceptance in a low-trust environment shaped by repeated reforms and economic instability. The literature still provides only limited attention to legitimacy as a practical condition of pension reform.

There is also limited research on how stakeholder perspectives themselves shape the development of pension reform. Much of the literature focuses on macroeconomic trends, fiscal projections, or institutional models, but less attention is given to how professionally informed actors assess the feasibility of reform measures in practice. This matters because pension reform does not take place in an abstract setting. It is influenced by the expectations, priorities, and perceived constraints of policymakers, regulators, insurers, and experts. By focusing on stakeholder perceptions, the present study addresses this gap and adds a more practice-oriented dimension to the literature.

Another gap concerns the conditional nature of support for private insurers. Existing discussions often treat the private sector either as a useful complement to public pensions or as a potential source of market risk and inequality. The literature less often examines the conditions under which support for private insurers becomes stronger or weaker. The present study suggests that this support is not unconditional. It depends on product transparency, simplicity, fairness, and regulatory credibility. This is important because it shows that the future role of private insurers in Greece is likely to depend not only on demographic pressure or market opportunity, but also on whether they are seen as trustworthy actors within a broader pension governance framework.

Finally, the literature remains limited in linking long-term demographic change with the practical sequencing of policy reform. While the pressures of ageing are well established, less attention has been paid to how reform measures should be introduced in practice if supplementary pension provision is to expand in a credible way. In the Greek case, this is especially relevant because trust, participation, and regulatory capacity are unlikely to develop at the same speed. The present study therefore suggests that future research should not only ask which reforms are desirable, but also in what order they are more likely to become effective and socially acceptable.

Chapter 3 RESEARCH METHODOLOGY

This chapter outlines the research methodology employed to examine the sustainability of the Greek pension system and the role of private insurers. Given the applied nature of the research, a survey-based approach is adopted to gather data from key stakeholders, including policymakers and insurance professionals. The research design is descriptive and cross-sectional, utilizing both qualitative and quantitative methods. This chapter discusses the philosophical underpinnings, sampling techniques, data collection methods, and ethical considerations that guided the investigation. It also details the strategies used to ensure the validity and reliability of the research findings.

3.1 Research Philosophy

The dissertation adopts a pragmatic research philosophy, which is particularly suited to survey-based research and applied managerial investigations. Pragmatism is grounded in the belief that research should be driven by the research question and what works best to address it, rather than strict adherence to a single philosophical tradition such as positivism or interpretivism. Pragmatists emphasise the practical consequences and usefulness of findings in real-world contexts, aligning with the purpose of this research to produce actionable insights for policymakers and industry practitioners in the Greek pension and insurance sectors (Kaushik & Walsh, 2019). According to contemporary discussions on research paradigms, pragmatism enables researchers to integrate diverse methods and perspectives to generate comprehensive solutions to complex social and organisational problems (Tanko, 2024).

In addition, the adoption of a pragmatic research philosophy reflects the specific expectations of a Doctor of Business Administration programme. DBA research is inherently practice-oriented and seeks to generate knowledge that is directly relevant to organisational and policy contexts. Rather than prioritising theory development for its own sake, DBA studies emphasise the application of existing theories and analytical frameworks to complex real-world problems. In this sense, pragmatism provides an appropriate philosophical foundation, as it allows methodological choices to be driven by practical relevance, feasibility, and the potential contribution to decision-making processes.

Pragmatism recognises that multiple realities and ways of knowing may coexist and that the research question should determine the methodological approach (research methods and strategies), not the other way around (Foster, 2023). This flexibility makes pragmatism especially appropriate for mixed and multimethod studies, where both quantitative and qualitative data contribute to a richer understanding of phenomena. As Elgeddawy and Abouraia (2024) highlight, pragmatism allows researchers to combine quantitative measures of patterns and relationships with qualitative insights about experiences and perceptions, enhancing the relevance and applicability of findings.

In the context of this thesis, the pragmatic philosophy supports the use of a survey instrument to collect attitudes and perceptions from stakeholders, while also enabling the interpretation of findings in light of broader systemic issues affecting the Greek pension system. It avoids the limitations of strict positivist paradigms, which prioritise only objective measurements, by acknowledging the value of stakeholder perspectives in understanding complex policy environments (Elder-Vass, 2022). At the same time, it maintains compatibility with quantitative analysis, as required for rigorous survey research, by incorporating structured data collection and statistical interpretation. This approach mirrors the core tenet of pragmatism, which is to leverage multiple methods and data sources in pursuit of solutions that are both empirically grounded and practically useful (Dube et al., 2024).

The research problem addressed in this research project further supports the use of a pragmatic stance. Pension system sustainability represents a policy challenge characterised by uncertainty, long time horizons, and multiple interacting stakeholders. Outcomes are influenced not only by economic and demographic factors, but also by regulatory design, institutional capacity, and behavioural responses. A pragmatic research philosophy acknowledges these complexities and avoids overly reductionist explanations. Instead, it enables a balanced assessment of trade-offs and policy options, recognising that effective solutions must be context-specific rather than universally optimal.

Furthermore, pragmatism aligns with the managerial focus of this dissertation. The study seeks not just to describe the current state of pension sustainability and insurance roles but to inform policy and strategic decisions. Pragmatism's emphasis on applying 'what works' connects directly with managerial research, which prioritises actionable recommendations over abstract theorizing (Kelly & Cordeiro, 2020). This philosophy encourages researchers to engage with the lived experiences of practitioners and policymakers while also drawing on quantitative evidence to support decision-making processes. In sum, the pragmatic philosophy ensures methodological coherence and practical relevance, enabling this study to bridge academic rigour with real-world applicability.

Pragmatism aligns perfectly with the DBA's practice-oriented philosophy, prioritizing actionable solutions to managerial problems over theoretical purity. This philosophical stance enables the study to generate decision-relevant insights for both policymakers and insurance executives facing demographic challenges.

3.2 Research Design

This dissertation relies on a cross-sectional survey design to examine how professionally involved stakeholders currently view the sustainability of the Greek pension system and the potential role of private insurers. Data were collected at one defined point in time. The study does not attempt to observe changes over time or to manipulate variables. Its focus lies on capturing existing perceptions within the institutional setting in which pension reform is currently debated.

The survey was structured to gather comparable responses from different stakeholder groups. Participants were asked to evaluate statements relating to demographic pressure, long-term sustainability, reform orientation, and the contribution of private insurers. These evaluations were recorded using standardised response formats, including agreement scales, in order to ensure consistency across respondents (Setia, 2016; Koo & Yang, 2025). The intention was not to construct an abstract methodological model, but to obtain a clear empirical overview of stakeholder positioning.

Because the research questions concern present attitudes rather than behavioural development over time, a cross-sectional approach is appropriate. It allows the examination of how professional background, experience, and institutional exposure relate to reform-related perceptions (Thomas, 2023; Wang & Cheng, 2020). The resulting analysis identifies observable associations within the dataset. These associations do not imply causality, but they help clarify how different stakeholder categories interpret pension sustainability challenges (Maier, 2023).

The choice of design also reflects practical considerations. A longitudinal study would require repeated measurement and extended observation periods. Such an approach would exceed the scope of this applied DBA project. The selected design therefore balances analytical clarity with feasibility.

Operationally, the research instrument consists of a structured questionnaire with predominantly closed-ended and attitudinal items. Closed-ended questions allow for systematic quantitative processing. Agreement scales capture the direction and strength of views concerning reform credibility, sustainability constraints, and trust in private insurers. The dataset supports descriptive statistics, correlation analysis, group comparison, and regression modelling. Within this framework, the cross-sectional survey provides a coherent empirical basis for addressing the dissertation's research questions and for developing policy-relevant conclusions.

The study should therefore be understood as a cross-sectional snapshot of informed stakeholder perceptions rather than as a direct forecast of future pension outcomes.

3.3 Population & Sampling

In this survey-based study, the population refers to individuals who are professionally involved in, or have substantive insight into, the Greek pension system and the role of private insurers within it. Rather than focusing on the general public, the study deliberately concentrates on stakeholders with direct institutional, professional, or analytical exposure to pension policy and insurance provision. The target population therefore consists of three main groups: public sector policymakers engaged in pension regulation, private insurance professionals responsible for pension-related products, and academics or pension experts specialising in retirement systems and economic policy. Clarifying this distinction between population and target population is important, as it frames how the findings should be interpreted within a policy and managerial context (Willie, 2024).

Given the heterogeneity of this stakeholder environment, the research design differentiated respondents across clearly defined stakeholder groups. The intention was to ensure that the key professional perspectives relevant to the research questions were included. The population was therefore organised according to sector and professional role in order to structure data collection and avoid over-reliance on a single stakeholder category. Differentiating stakeholder groups is analytically useful where subgroups may hold systematically different views regarding pension reform and the role of private insurers.

However, although the design was informed by a stratified logic, the achieved sample does not constitute a strictly stratified random sample in the statistical sense. Access to expert respondents in the Greek pension and insurance environment proved more limited than anticipated. As a result, the final sample reflects a structured but non-probability approach. It is therefore more accurate to describe the sampling strategy as a non-probability stakeholder sample with stratified features rather than a fully randomised stratified design.

The rationale behind organising the sample along stakeholder lines was primarily analytical rather than purely statistical. Dividing respondents by professional background allowed the study to compare perceptions across policy, insurance, and academic domains. This structure enhances interpretive depth, even if it does not guarantee population-level representativeness (DeYoreo, 2018). In this sense, the sampling strategy was designed to support meaningful insight into differences in attitudes and priorities, rather than to estimate national opinion parameters.

An initial target of approximately 200 respondents was considered appropriate for a multi-stakeholder quantitative study and would have allowed for stronger statistical inference and subgroup analysis (Ahmed, 2024). In practice, the final sample was smaller, reflecting the challenges of engaging specialised respondents in a relatively narrow professional field. While this reduces statistical power, it does not undermine the exploratory value of the data. The achieved sample remains sufficient for descriptive analysis and for identifying patterns relevant to the research questions.

It is also important to emphasise the applied orientation of this DBA research. The purpose of the survey was not to measure attitudes across the Greek population as a whole, but to capture informed perspectives from actors familiar with pension sustainability, regulatory structures, and private-sector dynamics. For this reason, the strength of the sample lies in the relevance and expertise of the respondents rather than in formal representativeness alone.

Accordingly, the findings derived from this sample should be interpreted as reflecting informed stakeholder judgement. They provide insight into how key professional groups perceive demographic pressure, pension adequacy risks, and the potential contribution of private insurers. They do not claim to represent the views of all Greek citizens. This distinction aligns with the applied logic of business and policy research, where contextual knowledge and domain expertise often provide greater explanatory value than large-scale population sampling.

Table 3.1: Target Population and Strata

Stratum	**Description**	**Characteristics**	**Sampling Frame**
Policy Makers	Government officials responsible for pension policy and reforms	Knowledgeable about pension system sustainability and policy decisions	Government departments, ministries, policy networks
Insurance Professionals	Executives, managers, and professionals in the private insurance sector	Expertise in pension products, insurance policies, and long-term retirement solutions	Insurance companies, industry associations, regulatory bodies
Pension Experts & Academics	Academics and researchers with expertise in pension systems and economics	Research-oriented, analytical, and well-versed in the theoretical aspects of pension sustainability	Academic institutions, think tanks, research organisations

The sampling process was organised around these stakeholder strata by first identifying suitable access points for each group, such as policy networks, professional associations, insurance-sector contacts, academic institutions, and research organisations. Where complete registries were not available, organisational directories and professional networks were used to approach potential respondents. As a result, the realised sample was structured by stakeholder category, but respondent inclusion depended partly on accessibility and availability rather than on strict random selection. This limits statistical representativeness, but it still allows the study to generate relevant insights into stakeholder perceptions across different domains connected to pension sustainability in Greece.

A further methodological point concerns the use of stakeholder perceptions as a central empirical source. In studies of pension reform, perceptions should not be treated as secondary or purely subjective material. This is particularly true where the research problem concerns institutional sustainability, reform feasibility, and the practical role of private actors within a changing policy environment. Questions of this kind are shaped not only by demographic projections or fiscal indicators, but also by how relevant actors interpret risks, constraints, and possible solutions. For this reason, stakeholder perceptions are not external to the problem under examination. They form part of the institutional reality through which pension reform is discussed, evaluated, and potentially implemented.

This point is especially relevant in the Greek context. Pension reform has taken place over a long period of fiscal adjustment, repeated policy change, and institutional sensitivity. Under such conditions, the attitudes of policymakers, insurance professionals, and pension experts matter because they influence how credible different reform pathways appear in practice. A technically coherent pension reform does not become feasible simply because it is economically rational in abstract terms. It must also be regarded as workable, legitimate, and governable by those involved in its design, communication, and implementation. The present study therefore treats stakeholder judgement as analytically relevant evidence rather than as a substitute for macroeconomic or demographic analysis.

This also helps explain why the study adopts a practice-oriented and exploratory logic. The purpose is not to test a single deterministic model of pension reform, nor to generate population-level estimates of public opinion. Instead, the aim is to identify patterns in how professionally relevant actors understand sustainability pressures, adequacy concerns, and the possible contribution of private insurers within the Greek pension system. This is consistent with the broader DBA orientation of the dissertation. In an applied doctoral context, the value of empirical work often lies in its ability to generate decision-relevant insight under real institutional constraints, even where the sample is specialised and the findings are context-bound.

The use of a structured survey remains appropriate within this logic. Standardised items make it possible to compare responses across stakeholder categories and to identify areas of convergence and divergence. At the same time, the interpretation of the results remains cautious. The study does not claim that stakeholder perceptions provide a complete representation of the pension system, nor that they displace the need for demographic, fiscal, or regulatory evidence. Rather, they complement these forms of evidence by showing how the central issues of the dissertation are perceived by actors with direct professional exposure to them.

This methodological position also clarifies how the limitations of the study should be understood. The non-probability nature of the sample and its relatively modest size restrict the scope for statistical generalisation. However, these constraints do not remove the value of the dataset for the purposes of the present research. The study is designed to provide structured insight into informed opinion within a specialised field, not to estimate national distributions of belief. In this sense, its contribution is interpretive and practice-relevant rather than population-representative. That distinction is important, because the dissertation is concerned with reform feasibility and institutional positioning as much as with formal system characteristics.

Taken together, this methodological approach is consistent with the research problem, the DBA orientation of the study, and the institutional complexity of the Greek pension environment. It allows the dissertation to combine quantitative structure with contextual sensitivity, while remaining explicit about the limits of inference. This provides a defensible basis for analysing how key stakeholder groups understand pension sustainability and the potential role of private insurers in a changing demographic setting.

3.4 Data Gathering Method

The data for this study were collected through a structured, self-administered online survey. The purpose of the survey was to obtain comparable assessments from stakeholders who are professionally connected to the Greek pension system and to the private insurance sector operating within it.

The choice of a survey-based design reflects the analytical objective of the dissertation. The research seeks to identify patterns in stakeholder perceptions regarding sustainability, adequacy, and the potential role of private insurers. A structured questionnaire allows these views to be captured in a consistent format, making responses directly comparable across professional groups (Bell et al., 2022).

Because the target respondents are policymakers, insurance professionals, and pension experts, an online format was considered appropriate. These groups are geographically dispersed and operate within different institutional settings. The digital format enabled broad access while keeping the data collection process manageable. It also allowed respondents to complete the questionnaire independently and at a time convenient to them, which is relevant when addressing specialised professional audiences (Dillman et al., 2014).

Importantly, the survey was designed as an instrument to collect structured professional judgement, not general public opinion. This distinction aligns with the applied orientation of the study and with the stakeholder-based sampling logic outlined in the previous section.

3.4.1. Survey Design and Content

The questionnaire consisted primarily of closed-ended items, including Likert-scale statements, multiple-choice questions, and background variables.

The survey structure followed established design principles to ensure clarity, internal consistency, and coherence between items (Fowler, 2002). Likert-scale statements were used to measure perceptions of demographic pressure, long-term sustainability, adequacy risks, confidence in reform measures, and the perceived importance of private insurers. The wording was intentionally neutral in order to avoid suggesting preferred answers.

In addition, categorical questions captured respondent characteristics such as sector affiliation, professional experience, and prior exposure to the Greek pension system. These variables were included to enable structured comparison across stakeholder groups during the analysis phase.

Care was taken to keep the overall questionnaire focused and proportionate. The number of items was limited to those directly connected to the research questions. The sequence of questions followed a logical progression from general sustainability assessments to more specific views on reform measures and private insurance solutions.

3.4.2. Distribution Channels

The survey was distributed using established online platforms, including Google Forms and Microsoft Forms. These tools allowed structured data collection and secure storage of responses.

Distribution took place through professional channels, including insurance-sector contacts, government-related networks, academic institutions, and relevant professional associations. This targeted approach is recommended when surveying expert populations, as response rates tend to be higher when invitations are channelled through recognised professional networks (Lavidas et al., 2022).

The invitation message clearly outlined the purpose of the study, indicated the expected completion time, and emphasised confidentiality and voluntary participation. Respondents were also offered access to a summary of the results upon request. Prior research suggests that such transparency can positively influence participation in professional samples (Holtom et al., 2022).

As discussed in Section 3.3, participation depended on accessibility and willingness to respond rather than on strict random selection. While this limits formal representativeness, it is consistent with the stakeholder-oriented design of the study and with its applied research focus.

3.4.3. Pilot Testing and Pre-Testing

Prior to full deployment, the survey instrument underwent pilot testing with a small sample (n = 20) representing the target strata (policy, insurance, academic expertise). Pilot testing assessed question clarity, survey length, technical functionality, and respondent understanding. This iterative review process aligns with best practices in survey research, which recommend pre-testing to identify ambiguous items and to refine instrument structure (Presser et al., 2004).

Pilot respondents also provided qualitative feedback on perceived relevance and clarity of items. Feedback was used to revise the instrument, reduce measurement error, and strengthen construct validity, critical steps in ensuring the survey accurately captures the intended concepts (Bradburn et al., 2004).

3.4.4. Data Collection Timeline

Data collection occurred over a six-week period following pilot revisions. The timeline was divided into three phases:

1. **Week 1–2:** Survey launch and initial invitations.
2. **Week 3–4:** Follow-up reminders to non-respondents and outreach via professional networks.
3. **Week 5–6:** Final push for responses and survey closure.

Regular monitoring of response rates enabled adaptive outreach strategies if particular strata (e.g., policymakers) were underrepresented, which is a recognised risk in expert surveys.

3.4.5. Data Management

All survey data were downloaded from the platform in secure, encrypted formats for analysis. Records were anonymised prior to processing to maintain confidentiality. Data cleaning included checks for incomplete responses and outliers, with guidelines established for handling partial completions consistent with quantitative research norms (Sharifnia et al., 2025).

In summary – the way this survey was designed and used fits the study's pragmatic philosophy. The goal was to get good responses, keep them meaningful, and make sure the data could answer the research questions. Pilot testing helped. So did targeted distribution and clear timelines.

3.5 Instrument

The main tool for collecting data was a structured survey. It was built to capture what stakeholders think, how they perceive things, and what their experience tells them – all focused on Greece's pension system and the role of private insurers. The design followed the research questions and the conceptual framework closely. That should help with both validity and reliability.

3.5.1. Survey Structure and Question Types

The survey comprises six sections, each addressing a specific dimension of the research questions. The instrument incorporates both structured quantitative items, yielding numerical data suitable for statistical analysis, and open-ended qualitative items, enabling respondents to articulate their perspectives in their own words. The following provides an overview of each section.

Section 1: Demographic and Professional Profile: This section includes closed-ended questions to capture essential demographic information about respondents, such as:

- Profession (e.g., Policymaker, Insurance Professional, Pension Expert/Academic)

- Years of experience in pension policy, insurance, or related fields
- Experience with Greek pension systems (Yes/No)

This data allows for subgroup comparisons and supports stratified analysis based on respondents' professional background.

Section 2: Perceptions on Greece's Pension System (Pay-As-You-Go Model): This section features Likert scale questions designed to assess stakeholders' views on the sustainability of Greece's pay-as-you-go pension system. Respondents were asked to rate their agreement with statements about:

- Long-term sustainability of the pension system
- Confidence in current and future pension reforms
- Perceived risks to pension sustainability

These questions align with Research Question 1 (RQ1), exploring stakeholder perceptions of the sustainability and adequacy of Greece's pension system.

Section 3: Role of Private Insurers in Supplementary Pensions: This section includes a combination of Likert scale items and multiple-choice questions aimed at understanding the role of private insurers in Greece's pension system. The focus is on:

- The perceived contribution of private insurers to retirement outcomes
- Barriers to the penetration of private pension products in Greece
- Confidence in the regulatory environment for private insurers

This section addresses Research Question 3 (RQ3), examining the perceived role of private insurers in contributing to pension sustainability and adequacy.

Section 4: Regulatory and Policy Environment: This section includes attitudinal and scenario-based questions that explore respondents' views on:

- Existing and proposed policy measures to strengthen pension sustainability
- The integration of private and public pension systems
- The role of international regulatory bodies (such as the EU and EIOPA) in shaping pension provisions

This section directly contributes to Research Questions 3 (RQ3) and Research Question 4 (RQ4), focusing on strategic recommendations for enhancing the resilience and sustainability of Greece's pension system.

Section 5: General Views on Pension Reforms and Sustainability: This section delves into broader perceptions regarding pension reforms and sustainability, including:

- The need for diversification of retirement income sources
- The role of private insurance products in addressing pension adequacy gaps
- Cross-border pension solutions within the EU

These items are mapped to Research Questions 2 (RQ2), 3 (RQ3), and 4 (RQ4), exploring adequacy concerns, the role of private insurers, and policy solutions for a sustainable pension future.

Section 6: The Future of the Pension System: This final section includes open-ended questions to capture forward-looking insights on:

- Potential changes needed to maintain a financially sustainable pension system
- The evolving role of private insurers in the pension system

- Barriers to the expansion of supplementary pensions in Greece and solutions to overcome these challenges

These open-ended questions aim to provide qualitative insights to supplement the quantitative data collected in earlier sections, helping to build a comprehensive view of the Greek pension system's future.

3.5.2. Alignment with Research Questions

The survey is structured to align with the four research questions (RQ1-RQ4) and the main research question (MRQ):

- Demographic items allow for cross-sectional analysis of how background factors influence perceptions, supporting a deeper understanding of how different stakeholder groups view the pension system.
- Perceptions of pension sustainability provide data on stakeholders' views of current and future challenges facing Greece's pension system, addressing the Main Research Question (MRQ) and RQ1.
- Private insurer-related items examine the perceived role and effectiveness of private insurers in enhancing Greece's pension system, directly addressing RQ3.
- Regulatory and policy environment questions allow respondents to offer insights into policy recommendations, addressing RQ4 regarding the integration of private and public pension mechanisms and the role of international regulatory bodies.
- General views on reforms provide information on future trends, pension adequacy concerns, retirement income gaps, policy recommendations, and cross-border pension solutions, which informed RQ2, RQ3 and RQ4.

This alignment ensures that the instrument captures comprehensive, relevant data to answer all research questions.

3.5.3. Validation and Expert Review

To ensure content validity, the instrument underwent review by a panel of experts, including academic supervisors and pension system researchers. Expert review helps confirm that survey items are appropriate, unambiguous, and representative of the constructs being measured (Haynes, Richard & Kubany, 1995). Modifications were made based on expert feedback before pilot testing.

3.5.4. Pilot Testing

As outlined in Section 3.4, pilot testing with a small sample (n = 20) was used to assess item clarity, completion time, and technical issues. Cognitive interviewing techniques were also used with pilot participants to identify misunderstood items. Pilot data were further used for preliminary reliability testing (e.g., Cronbach's alpha) for scale items, thereby supporting internal consistency (Tavakol & Dennick, 2011).

3.5.5. Instrument Integrity

Throughout survey development, careful attention was paid to question wording, order effects, and response format to minimise measurement error. Standardised response scales support statistical analysis and comparability across strata. The result is an instrument that yields reliable, valid data aligned with the study's objectives and capable of informing evidence-based recommendations for pension policy and managerial practice.

Table 3.2 summarises the alignment between the research questions, key variables, survey sections, and analytical methods employed in this study.

Table 3.2: Research Design Alignment

Research Question	Key Variables	Survey Section	Analysis Method
RQ 1	Perceptions of demographic pressure and long-term sustainability of the Greek pension system	Sections 2 and 4	Descriptive statistics, reliability analysis, correlation analysis, regression analysis
RQ 2	Perceptions of pension adequacy risks and future retirement income gaps	Sections 2 and 5	Descriptive statistics, correlation analysis, group comparison, regression analysis
RQ 3	Perceived role of private insurers, annuities, and longevity-risk solutions	Sections 3, 5 and 6	Descriptive statistics, reliability analysis, correlation analysis
RQ 4	Perceived policy and regulatory measures for expanding supplementary pensions while maintaining trust and fairness	Sections 4, 5 and 6	Descriptive statistics, correlation analysis, regression analysis

3.6 Validity & Reliability

Ensuring validity and reliability is important for showing that the empirical findings are credible and methodologically sound. In this study, these issues are considered in practical rather than purely textbook terms. The main concern is whether the survey instrument captured stakeholder perceptions of pension sustainability and the possible role of private insurers in a clear and consistent way.

Reliability mainly concerns whether items intended to measure similar ideas produced responses that moved in a reasonably consistent direction. For the Likert-scale blocks on sustainability perceptions and insurer relevance, internal consistency measures such as Cronbach's alpha were used as an appropriate check of whether the grouped items worked together as expected (Hossan et al., 2025). If items that are meant to reflect the same concept point in very different directions, interpretation becomes less secure. For that reason, particular attention was given to wording, clarity, and conceptual consistency during questionnaire development.

Validity was considered in relation to how closely the survey items reflected the theoretical discussion presented in Chapter 2. Rather than treating validity as an abstract methodological label, the emphasis here is on alignment between concepts and measurement. Items on demographic pressure, adequacy concerns, reform confidence, and insurer capacity were derived from themes identified in the literature (Karnia, 2024). Construct validity is supported where the response patterns are theoretically plausible, for example where perceptions of ageing pressure are associated with concerns about long-term sustainability (Alabbasi et al., 2025). Such relationships do not prove the concepts perfectly, but they do provide some support for the way the main ideas were operationalised in the survey.

Although the study is primarily quantitative, some broader quality considerations also remain relevant. Clear documentation of sampling choices, item construction, and analytical steps helps strengthen transparency and dependability (Noble & Smith, 2025). The findings were also interpreted alongside institutional reports and secondary evidence, so that the statistical results were not treated in isolation from their wider policy context (Hossan et al., 2025).

Before the survey was distributed, the questionnaire was reviewed and refined in order to reduce ambiguity and make sure that the terminology would be understood in a similar way by policymakers, insurance professionals, and academic respondents. This does not remove measurement error entirely, but it improves confidence that responses reflect considered stakeholder judgement rather than misunderstanding. Taken together, these steps support the overall robustness of the empirical analysis without claiming more precision than the instrument can realistically provide.

3.7 Ethical Considerations

Ethical issues in this study arise mainly from the professional profile of the respondents and from the sensitivity of pension reform as a policy issue in Greece. Although the survey did not involve vulnerable groups, it did involve participants working in policy, pensions, and financial institutions, where confidentiality and careful data handling are particularly important.

Participation was voluntary. Respondents were informed about the academic purpose of the study, the approximate time needed to complete the questionnaire, and the fact that results would be used only in aggregated form. This approach is consistent with basic ethical principles such as informed consent and respect for participants (Akter et al., 2025). No identifying information was reported in the analysis, and responses were treated anonymously in order to reduce any risk of professional consequences for participants expressing critical or sensitive views.

Data were collected through secure online platforms, and access to raw responses was restricted to the researcher. Ethical research governance frameworks, including the principles reflected in the Declaration of Helsinki (World Medical Association, 2024 revision), emphasise the importance of transparency, proportionality, and participant protection. While originally developed for medical contexts, the underlying standards of disclosure, risk minimisation, and accountability remain applicable in social science research (Bhandari, 2024).

By embedding these safeguards into the research process, the study aims to balance analytical inquiry with professional responsibility, ensuring that stakeholder engagement in a policy-sensitive domain is conducted in a respectful and methodologically sound manner.

Research ethics governance frameworks, such as the World Medical Association's Declaration of Helsinki (2024 revision), emphasise that researchers must prioritise participant welfare above scientific objectives, disclose all relevant risks and benefits, and adhere to both local and international ethical standards (World Medical Association, 2024). Obtaining ethics committee or Institutional Review Board (IRB) approval prior to data collection formalises this commitment, ensuring a structured assessment of participant protection, methodological rigour, and risk–benefit balance.

In addition, researchers must uphold integrity and transparency in reporting results, avoiding misconduct such as fabrication, falsification, and plagiarism. Ethical research practice also involves declaring conflicts of interest and articulating procedures to safeguard data privacy and anonymity, thereby reinforcing public trust in research findings and scholarly outputs (Ali et al., 2025).

3.8 Methodological Limitations

This cross-sectional survey design captures perceptions at a single point in time, limiting causal inference. Findings are context-specific to Greece and may have limited generalizability. Self-reported data carries common method bias risk, mitigated through procedural remedies (expert validation, pilot testing) but not eliminated.

A further methodological limitation concerns the sampling approach. Although the study was designed around stakeholder strata, the final achieved sample cannot be regarded as a fully stratified random sample in a strict statistical sense. Access to respondents depended partly on professional networks, organisational contacts, and the practical availability of expert participants. The realised sample is therefore more accurately understood as a non-probability sample with stratified features. This limits strict statistical representativeness and means that the findings should be interpreted as exploratory and practice-oriented rather than fully generalisable to the wider population.

Nevertheless, this limitation is consistent with the exploratory and applied purpose of the study. The research does not aim to produce population-level estimates of public opinion, but rather to examine informed stakeholder perceptions regarding pension sustainability, demographic pressure, and the potential role of private insurers. For this reason, the sample remains appropriate for identifying patterns, relationships, and managerial implications relevant to the Greek pension and insurance context. The findings should therefore be interpreted with caution, but they remain valuable for understanding how key stakeholder groups perceive the strategic and policy conditions under which supplementary pension provision may develop.

A further limitation relates to the nature of the evidence generated by the survey itself. The study captures informed stakeholder assessments rather than observed behavioural outcomes or longitudinal institutional change. This means that the findings are better understood as evidence of how relevant actors interpret the sustainability and adequacy challenges of the Greek pension system, rather than as direct evidence of how households, firms, or public institutions will necessarily behave over time. In a policy field such as pensions, this distinction is important. Stakeholder perceptions can help identify where concerns, expectations, and perceived constraints are concentrated, but they do not on their own establish whether future reforms will be politically adopted, socially accepted, or operationally successful.

A related limitation is that the survey design cannot fully capture the variation that may exist within stakeholder categories themselves. For example, insurance professionals, policymakers, and academic experts may each contain internal differences in experience, sectoral exposure, and institutional perspective. While the study recognises these broad groupings as analytically useful, the relatively modest sample size does not allow for a highly granular comparison of sub-groups. As a result, the empirical analysis is better suited to identifying broad patterns of judgement than to making fine distinctions within each professional category.

There is also a limit arising from the scope of the study's evidence base. The dissertation does not attempt a full actuarial valuation of pension liabilities, nor does it model future replacement rates or investment outcomes in a formal forecasting framework. These issues are clearly relevant to the long-term future of pension provision, but they fall outside the empirical design adopted here. The contribution of the study therefore lies less in forecasting exact pension outcomes and more in clarifying how demographic pressure, adequacy concerns, and the possible role of private insurers are understood by professionally relevant stakeholders within the current Greek institutional setting.

These limitations do not invalidate the study, but they do shape the level at which its conclusions should be read. The dissertation is most credible when interpreted as an applied and exploratory contribution to understanding pension reform feasibility, institutional perceptions, and the governance conditions under which supplementary provision may expand. Its findings are therefore better used to inform judgement, debate, and further inquiry than as a basis for strong predictive claims.

The findings should therefore be interpreted as exploratory and practice-focused, with emphasis on stakeholder-informed insight rather than statistical representativeness.

It is acknowledged that the original framing of RQ1 implied a long-term analytical horizon (2050–2070) that exceeds what a cross-sectional stakeholder survey can directly address. The revised RQ1 therefore focuses on stakeholder assessments of sustainability constraints rather than on longitudinal projections. The empirical findings are interpreted as reflecting current practitioner perceptions rather than as actuarial projections or longitudinal forecasts.

3.9 Methodological Positioning within Applied DBA Research

This research follows the applied orientation of a Doctor of Business Administration programme. The intention was not to generate statistically representative results for the Greek population as a whole, but to examine how professionally relevant stakeholders understand the current sustainability pressures and the potential role of supplementary pension provision.

Given the institutional complexity of the Greek pension system, the study focused on respondents who are directly or indirectly involved in pension policy, regulation, or insurance practice. The sampling approach therefore emphasised professional relevance and contextual knowledge rather than probabilistic representativeness. In an applied policy setting, such informed perspectives are particularly valuable when the objective is to understand feasibility, constraints, and governance conditions.

The achieved sample size of 68 respondents reflects the practical limits of accessing specialised expert groups. While this naturally restricts the scope for broad statistical generalisation, it does not reduce the interpretative value of the findings. The statistical procedures were used to identify observable relationships and patterns within the dataset. They are interpreted as exploratory indicators rather than as predictive models.

Accordingly, the results should be read in conjunction with the demographic, fiscal, and institutional analysis presented in earlier chapters. The empirical component supports structured reflection on stakeholder perceptions and policy implications, rather than claiming universal inference.

This positioning is consistent with the purpose of a DBA dissertation, which aims to connect analytical reasoning with managerial and policy relevance. By combining stakeholder-based empirical evidence with contextual analysis, the study contributes to a more practice-oriented understanding of pension system development in Greece.

Chapter 4 FINDINGS AND ANALYSIS

This chapter presents and interprets the empirical findings of the study on the future of pension systems in Greece and the role of private insurers in the context of demographic change. The analysis is based on survey data from 68 respondents drawn from a range of professional backgrounds relevant to pensions, insurance, public policy, finance, and related fields. Consistent with the methodology outlined in Chapter 3, the chapter combines descriptive and inferential statistical analysis to address the study's main research question and the four subsidiary research questions.

The main research question asked:

How do professionally relevant stakeholders assess the implications of demographic change for the sustainability and adequacy of Greece's pension system, and under which conditions can supplementary funded solutions supported by private insurers contribute to sustainable retirement income provision?

The four subsidiary questions were:

RQ1: How do professionally relevant stakeholders assess the long-term sustainability constraints that demographic change is likely to place on Greece's pay-as-you-go pension system?

RQ2: How do professionally relevant stakeholders perceive current and emerging pension adequacy risks in Greece as population ageing progresses and earlier pension reforms mature?

RQ3: Which insurer capabilities and product mechanisms do professionally relevant stakeholders consider most relevant for supporting supplementary retirement income provision in Greece?

RQ4: Which policy and regulatory measures do professionally relevant stakeholders consider most important for expanding supplementary pensions while protecting consumers and maintaining trust?

To answer these questions, the chapter is organised into six main sections. First, respondent characteristics are presented to establish the composition of the sample. Second, descriptive statistics are analysed to identify broad attitudinal patterns. Third, reliability analysis assesses the internal consistency of the key scales used in the study. Fourth, correlation analysis examines the relationships between central variables. Fifth, an independent samples t-test is used to compare responses between those with and without prior experience of Greek pension systems. Sixth, two regression models are presented to explore predictors of sustainability perceptions and support for private insurance solutions.

The chapter does not merely report numerical results. It also interprets them in light of the dissertation's theoretical focus, research questions, and wider literature reviewed in Chapter 2. In doing so, it seeks to move beyond description and to explain what the findings imply for the future of Greek pension reform, the role of private insurers, and the feasibility of a more robust multi-pillar pension model.

4.1 Respondent Profile

The first step in the analysis is to understand who responded to the survey. This is important because the value of the findings depends not only on the number of responses, but also on whether respondents are sufficiently relevant to the subject of pension sustainability and reform.

4.1.1. Profession of respondents

Table 4.1 presents the professional profile of the respondents.

Table 4.1: Respondents by profession (N = 68)

Profession	Frequency	Percent
Academic Management	3	4.4
All of the above	2	2.9
Controlling Expert in Insurance	3	4.4
Economist	4	5.9
Insurance Professional	27	39.7
Legal Advisor	1	1.5
Pension Expert/Academic	9	13.2
Policymaker	6	8.8
Postgraduate Finance Student	2	2.9
Public servant	4	5.9
Software Engineer	6	8.8
Team Leader at Pension Department of an Occupational Insurance Fund	1	1.5
Total	**68**	**100.0**

As shown in Table 4.1, the largest single group in the sample is Insurance Professionals, who account for 39.7% of all respondents. This is followed by Pension Experts/Academics at 13.2% and Policymakers at 8.8%. Other respondents include economists, public servants, academic managers, and professionals from related technical or financial fields.

This composition is meaningful for the aims of the study. Because the dissertation focuses partly on the potential role of private insurers, it is valuable to have a strong representation from respondents with insurance-sector knowledge. At the same time, the presence of policymakers, pension experts, academics, and public servants helps avoid reducing the analysis to a purely market-oriented viewpoint. The sample, therefore, contains a mix of public, private, and expert perspectives, although it is fair to note that it is more heavily weighted toward the insurance and professional practice side than toward public administration alone.

Figure 4.1 graphically illustrates this distribution. The chart shows clearly that insurance-related respondents dominate the sample, while other professional groups are smaller and more dispersed. This matters when interpreting later findings, especially on the role of private insurers, because strong support for supplementary funded arrangements could partly reflect the occupational composition of the respondents. However, as later analyses show, support for private insurance is not limited to one group alone.

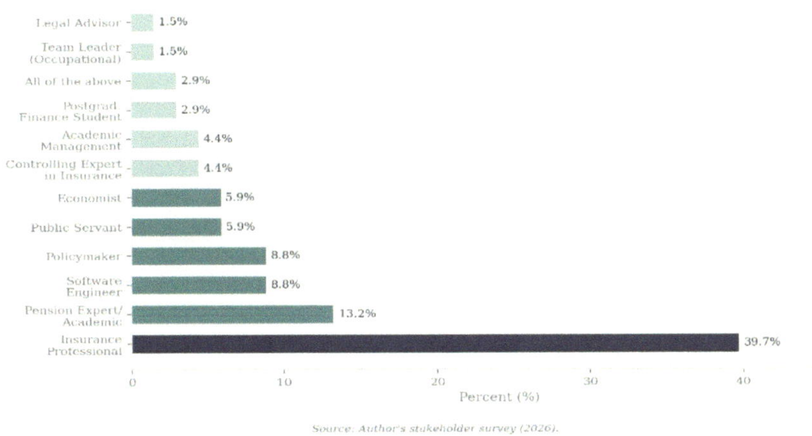

Figure 4.1 Distribution of respondents by profession

Figure 4.1 shows the percentage distribution of the survey sample across professional categories. Insurance professionals form the largest category, followed by pension experts/academics and policymakers. The chart illustrates the practice-oriented composition of the sample.

4.1.2. Years of Experience

Table 4.2 presents respondents' years of experience in pension policy, insurance, or related fields.

Table 4.2: Respondents by years of experience (N = 68)

Years of experience	**Frequency**	**Percent**
0–5 years	22	32.4
6–10 years	9	13.2
11–20 years	14	20.6
21+ years	23	33.8
Total	**68**	**100.0**

The sample includes respondents with different levels of experience. The largest group has 21 or more years of experience (33.8%). This is followed by respondents with 0–5 years of experience (32.4%). Respondents with 11–20 years account for 20.6%, while those with 6–10 years account for 13.2%.

Figure 4.2 shows this distribution. The results indicate that the sample includes both more experienced and less experienced respondents. It is therefore not concentrated in only one experience category.

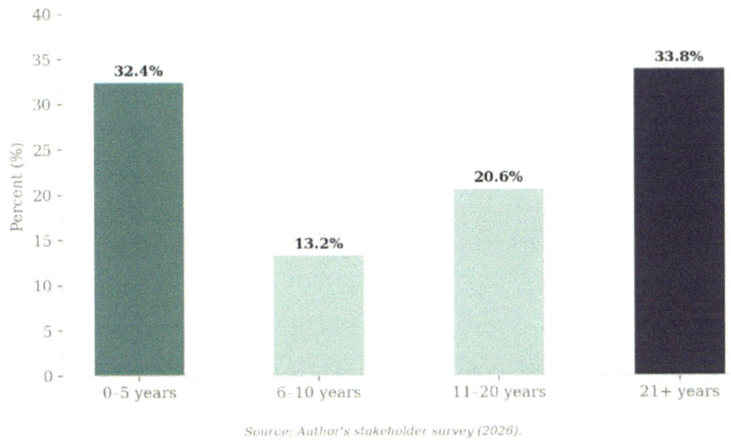

Figure 4.2 Respondents by years of experience

Figure 4.2 shows the proportion of respondents according to years of experience in pension policy, insurance, or related fields. The chart indicates a balanced sample between early-career and very experienced respondents, with a smaller middle-range group.

4.1.3. Prior experience with Greek Pension Systems

Respondents were also asked whether they had previously worked with pension systems in Greece.

Table 4.3: Prior experience with Greek pension systems (N = 68)

Response	**Frequency**	**Percent**
No	43	63.2
Yes	25	36.8
Total	**68**	**100.0**

As shown in Table 4.3, a majority of respondents (63.2%) had not previously worked with pension systems in Greece, while 36.8% reported that they had. This finding is important for interpretation. On the one hand, it indicates that not all respondents are direct insiders to the Greek pension system. On the other hand, this is not necessarily a weakness, because the dissertation also concerns broader insurance, demographic, and policy questions that are not confined to one national administrative experience. Moreover, the comparison between those with and without direct Greek pension experience becomes analytically useful later in the chapter when group differences are explored. Figure 4.3 shows that the sample contains a clear majority without direct Greek-system experience, but a substantial minority with such experience.

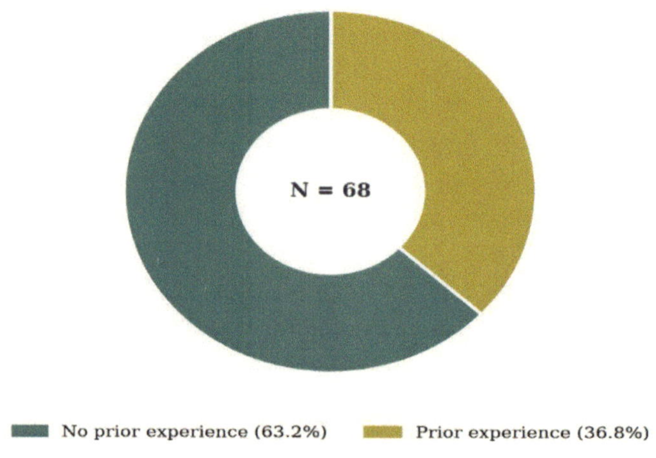

Figure 4.3 Prior experience with Greek pension systems

Figure 4.3 shows that most respondents had not previously worked with Greek pension systems, while just over one-third had direct prior experience. This provides a basis for later comparison of perception differences.

4.2 Descriptive Statistics

Descriptive statistics provide an overview of central tendencies across the survey items. They reveal where respondents show stronger agreement or disagreement and help identify broad patterns before inferential analysis is undertaken.

Table 4.4: Descriptive statistics for key survey items

Survey item	**N**	**Mean**	**Std. Deviation**
Greece's pension system is currently sustainable in the long term	68	2.53	1.029
The current pay-as-you-go pension system in Greece is adequate to meet the future needs of retirees	68	2.28	1.157
Greece's pension system is under significant pressure due to the ageing population	68	4.34	0.589
Demographic ageing will continue to strain Greece's pension system over the next 50 years	68	4.31	0.652
The current pension reforms will not be enough to ensure long-term sustainability	68	3.78	0.928
Private insurers can play an important role in supporting Greece's pension system	68	4.01	0.801
Private insurance products like annuities can help reduce the risk of outliving retirement savings	68	3.84	0.563
There is sufficient demand for supplementary pension products in Greece	63	2.87	1.211

Survey item	**N**	**Mean**	**Std. Deviation**
Private insurers should focus on designing simple and transparent pension products for Greek citizens	68	4.43	0.698
The role of private insurers in pension provision is essential to reduce the pressure on the public pension system	68	3.87	0.845
Private insurers should focus on providing products that address longevity risks in the Greek pension system	67	4.01	0.685
The Greek government is doing enough to support the development of supplementary pension schemes	68	2.63	0.913
Greece needs to reform its tax incentives for private pension savings to increase participation	68	4.24	0.964
There should be greater integration between public and private pension systems to ensure retirement security	68	4.01	0.801
Policy measures such as auto-enrolment in supplementary pension schemes will help expand participation	68	3.93	0.434
Consumer protection laws should be strengthened to ensure that private pension products are fair and transparent	68	4.25	0.904
A Pan-European Personal Pension Product (PEPP) could provide a viable solution to Greece's supplementary pension challenges	68	3.94	0.896
The role of international regulatory bodies, such as the EU and EIOPA, should be	68	4.09	0.787

Survey item	N	Mean	Std. Deviation
enhanced to ensure fair pension provisions across Europe			
Greece should prioritize pension sustainability over short-term fiscal relief	68	4.09	0.893
Pension reforms should focus on ensuring that future retirees have adequate income despite demographic challenges	68	4.37	0.644
Greece's pension system needs to diversify its sources of retirement income to ensure long-term sustainability	68	4.19	0.758
The introduction of private insurance products will be essential to address future pension adequacy gaps in Greece	68	3.93	0.903
Greece should explore cross-border pension solutions within the EU to strengthen retirement income provision	68	3.79	0.873

4.2.1. Perceptions of pension sustainability and adequacy

The first two items capture respondents' assessments of the Greek pension system's current long-term sustainability and future adequacy. These produce relatively low means: 2.53 for sustainability and 2.28 for adequacy. Both scores fall below the midpoint of the five-point scale, indicating that respondents generally do not view the Greek pension system as sustainable in the long term, nor do they believe that the existing pay-as-you-go structure is adequate to meet future retirement needs.

This is an important finding because it establishes the empirical foundation for the dissertation as a whole. The study began from the premise that Greece's pension system faces structural pressure from ageing, fiscal constraints, and limited diversification. The descriptive results strongly support that premise. Respondents do not appear confident that the present system, in its current form, can adequately meet the needs of future retirees.

These findings speak directly to RQ1 and RQ2. For RQ1, the low sustainability mean suggests that respondents see the system as constrained under existing institutional arrangements. For RQ2, the low adequacy mean signals concern about emerging or future pension adequacy gaps.

4.2.2. Perceptions of demographic pressure

Two items measure the degree to which respondents see demographic ageing as a key challenge. These receive some of the highest means in the dataset: 4.34 for the statement that Greece's pension system is under significant pressure due to the ageing population, and 4.31 for the statement that demographic ageing will continue to strain the system over the next 50 years.

These high scores indicate a broad and strong consensus among respondents that demographic change is not a peripheral issue but a central structural pressure. In other words, respondents do not view pension strain as temporary or cyclical. They see it as deeply tied to long-run population dynamics. This aligns closely with the literature reviewed in Chapter 2, which highlighted rising old-age dependency ratios, low fertility, and longer life expectancy as core drivers of pension stress in Greece.

The item on whether current reforms will not be enough to ensure long-term sustainability also records a relatively high mean (3.78), suggesting that respondents are not persuaded that recent or current reforms fully resolve the problem. Together, these three items indicate a fairly coherent perception: demographic change is severe, it will persist, and current reforms may not be sufficient.

This is highly relevant to RQ1, because it suggests that the sustainability constraints facing Greece's pay-as-you-go system are perceived as structural, long-term, and only partially addressed by existing reform measures.

4.2.3. Perceptions of private insurers and retirement products

The set of items relating to private insurers produces consistently positive results. Respondents strongly agree that private insurers can play an important role in supporting Greece's pension system (Mean = 4.01), and they also agree that insurers are essential to reducing pressure on the public pension system (Mean = 3.87). The idea that private insurance products will be essential to address future pension adequacy gaps also attracts strong support (Mean = 3.93).

Respondents are particularly positive about the design role of insurers. The highest mean in the entire dataset is for the statement that insurers should focus on designing simple and transparent pension products (Mean = 4.43). This is a significant result. It suggests that support for private insurers is not unconditional. Respondents do not merely endorse greater market participation in abstract terms. They place emphasis on product clarity, usability, and trustworthiness. Similarly, there is strong support for products that address longevity risks (Mean = 4.01) and for annuities as a tool to reduce the risk of outliving retirement savings (Mean = 3.84).

These findings are central to RQ3, which asks which insurer capabilities and product mechanisms can support sustainable retirement income in Greece. The descriptive data suggests three recurring themes:

first, respondents recognise a meaningful role for private insurers; second, they view protection against longevity risk as important; third, they want supplementary products to be simple, transparent, and credible.

4.2.4. Perceptions of policy and regulatory support

The policy-related items reveal two interesting patterns. First, respondents are quite supportive of reform measures such as tax incentives (Mean = 4.24), greater integration between public and private systems (Mean = 4.01), auto-enrolment (Mean = 3.93), stronger consumer protection laws (Mean = 4.25), and the enhancement of EU/EIOPA roles (Mean = 4.09). These means show broad support for policy change and institutional strengthening.

Second, respondents do not believe that the Greek government is currently doing enough to support the development of supplementary pension schemes (Mean = 2.63). This is a notable contrast. Respondents support reform in principle, but they are less satisfied with existing government support in practice.

The item on whether Greece should prioritise pension sustainability over short-term fiscal relief also receives strong support (Mean = 4.09), indicating that respondents favour a longer-term strategic approach over narrow short-run fiscal management. Likewise, there is substantial support for ensuring adequate future retiree income despite demographic pressures (Mean = 4.37) and for diversifying retirement income sources (Mean = 4.19).

These results are highly relevant to RQ4. They suggest that respondents support a package of measures that includes fiscal incentives, governance reform, stronger consumer protection, institutional integration, and potentially wider European frameworks. However, the low score on current government support also suggests a perceived implementation gap.

4.3 Reliability Analysis

Reliability analysis was conducted to test whether items grouped into broader conceptual scales display acceptable internal consistency. Cronbach's alpha was used for this purpose.

Table 4.5: Reliability analysis

Scale	Cronbach's Alpha	Number of items
Demographic Pressure	0.742	3
Private Insurance Role	0.870	3
Policy-related items	0.400	4

The Demographic Pressure scale, consisting of three items related to ageing pressure, future strain, and reform insufficiency, recorded an alpha of 0.742. This indicates acceptable to good internal consistency. The items appear to capture a reasonably coherent construct, namely the perception that demographic change is exerting a sustained and significant pressure on the Greek pension system.

The Private Insurance Role scale produced an alpha of 0.870, which indicates strong internal consistency. This is an important result because it shows that support for private insurers is not fragmented across the three items used. Rather, respondents who see private insurers as important also tend to see them as essential for relieving public pressure and for addressing future adequacy gaps. This reinforces the substantive relevance of RQ3 and gives confidence that attitudes toward private insurance form a relatively unified perspective within the sample.

By contrast, the four policy-related items (tax incentives, system integration, auto-enrolment, and consumer protection) produced a Cronbach's alpha of 0.400, indicating low internal consistency. The low Cronbach΄s alpha indicates that these items should not be interpreted as a robust unified scale. Methodologically, this is understandable, as the items represent conceptually distinct policy instruments that respondents may not perceive as one single dimension. A respondent may support stronger consumer protection while being more cautious about auto-enrolment, or may favour tax incentives without fully endorsing deeper system integration. For this reason, these policy items are treated in the subsequent analysis as analytically distinct indicators rather than as a single aggregated “policy-related items”.

4.4 Correlation Analysis

Correlation analysis was conducted to examine the relationships between the central variables linked to sustainability, adequacy, demographic change, private insurers, and policy reform. The correlation coefficients are reproduced in Table 4.6.

Table 4.6: Selected Pearson correlations among key variables

Variable pair	**r**	**Significance**
Sustainability ↔ Adequacy	0.777	$p < 0.01$
Sustainability ↔ Ageing pressure	-0.325	$p < 0.01$
Sustainability ↔ Future demographic strain	-0.403	$p < 0.01$
Sustainability ↔ Diversification need	-0.342	$p < 0.01$
Ageing pressure ↔ Future demographic strain	0.734	$p < 0.01$
Ageing pressure ↔ Tax reform need	0.489	$p < 0.01$
Ageing pressure ↔ Diversification need	0.488	$p < 0.01$
Future demographic strain ↔ Private insurers essential	0.400	$p < 0.01$
Future demographic strain ↔ Tax reform need	0.405	$p < 0.01$

Variable pair	r	Significance
Future demographic strain ↔ Diversification need	0.392	p < 0.01
Future demographic strain ↔ Private insurance essential	0.343	p < 0.01
Private insurers important ↔ Insurers essential	0.687	p < 0.01
Private insurers important ↔ Tax reform need	0.537	p < 0.01
Private insurers important ↔ Diversification need	0.487	p < 0.01
Private insurers important ↔ Private insurance essential	0.621	p < 0.01
Insurers essential ↔ Private insurance essential	0.770	p < 0.01
Tax reform need ↔ Diversification need	0.571	p < 0.01
Tax reform need ↔ Private insurance essential	0.449	p < 0.01
Diversification need ↔ Private insurance essential	0.479	p < 0.01

The correlation results provide an initial indication of how respondents connect the main dimensions of the study. Overall, the pattern suggests that perceptions of demographic pressure, pension sustainability, and the role of private insurers are not viewed as separate issues. Instead, respondents appear to associate long-term demographic strain with the need for diversification, tax reform, and stronger supplementary pension provision. This is important for the interpretation of the findings, because it suggests that support for private insurance solutions does not emerge in isolation, but is linked to broader concerns about the future capacity of the public pension system. At the same time, the correlations should not be interpreted as evidence of causality. They show statistically significant associations between perceptions, but they do not prove that one perception directly causes another. The results therefore provide a useful basis for further interpretation in the following subsections and in the regression analysis

4.4.1. Sustainability, adequacy, and demographic pressure

The strongest correlation involving the two core system-evaluation items is between perceived sustainability and perceived adequacy ($r = 0.777$, $p < 0.01$). This indicates that respondents who believe the Greek pension system is more sustainable also tend to believe it is more adequate for future retirees. Conversely, those who rate it as unsustainable also tend to see it as inadequate. This is conceptually intuitive and reinforces the close connection between fiscal/systemic sustainability and benefit adequacy in pension debates.

Perceived sustainability is negatively correlated with both ageing pressure ($r = -0.325$, $p < 0.01$) and future demographic strain ($r = -0.403$, $p < 0.01$). This means that the more respondents recognise demographic pressure, the less likely they are to believe that the current system is sustainable in the long term. A similar pattern is visible with diversification need ($r = -0.342$, $p < 0.01$). Those who believe diversification is necessary are less likely to think the current system is sustainable.

These relationships directly support RQ1. They show that respondents do not treat demographic change as an abstract future issue. Rather, they associate it with present doubts about the long-term viability of the Greek pension model.

4.4.2. Demographic pressure and reform orientation

The correlation between ageing pressure and future demographic strain is very strong ($r = 0.734$, $p < 0.01$), which confirms the coherence of the demographic pressure construct identified in the reliability analysis. Respondents who see pressure today also expect it to continue over time.

Ageing pressure is also positively correlated with the perceived need for tax reform ($r = 0.489$, $p < 0.01$) and the perceived need to diversify retirement income sources ($r = 0.488$, $p < 0.01$). The positive correlations indicate that demographic concern is associated not merely with pessimism, but with a reform orientation. Respondents who perceive stronger demographic strain are more likely to endorse changes that expand supplementary mechanisms or reduce exclusive reliance on the public pillar.

This is important for both RQ1 and RQ4. It implies that the perceived demographic challenge creates support for policy innovation, not just alarm.

4.4.3. Private insurers and adequacy solutions

One of the most important findings in the dataset concerns the interrelationships among the private insurance variables. The belief that private insurers can play an important role is strongly correlated with the view that their role is essential to reduce pressure on the public pension system ($r = 0.687$, $p < 0.01$). Even more strongly, the latter is correlated with the view that private insurance products will be essential to address future adequacy gaps ($r = 0.770$, $p < 0.01$). The direct relationship between insurers' importance and the adequacy-gap item is also strong ($r = 0.621$, $p < 0.01$).

These results provide some of the clearest empirical support for RQ3. They show that respondents link the strategic role of private insurers not only to system support in general, but specifically to the future adequacy problem. In other words, private insurers are not seen simply as auxiliary commercial actors; they are perceived as part of the solution to an emerging retirement-income gap.

4.4.4. Policy measures and private insurance

Support for private insurers is significantly associated with support for tax reform ($r = 0.537$, $p < 0.01$) and diversification of retirement income ($r = 0.487$, $p < 0.01$). In addition, support for tax reform is strongly associated with support for diversification (r = 0.571, $p < 0.01$) and moderately associated with the view that private insurance is essential for future adequacy (r = 0.449, $p < 0.01$).

These results suggest that respondents view private insurance and public policy as complementary rather than competing spheres. The private insurance role appears strongest where respondents also favour supportive policy conditions such as tax incentives and broader diversification. This has important implications for RQ4: the data indicate that private insurers are not viewed as substitutes for the public system in an unregulated market sense. Rather, their role is seen as more viable when combined with enabling policy frameworks.

4.5 Group Comparison: Independent Samples t-test

To explore whether direct prior experience with Greek pension systems influences perceptions of private insurers, an independent samples t-test was conducted using the item: "Private insurers can play an important role in supporting Greece's pension system."

Table 4.7: Group means for the t-test

Prior experience with Greek pension systems	N	Mean	Std. Deviation
Yes	25	3.76	1.052
No	43	4.16	0.574

The mean score is lower among respondents with prior Greek pension-system experience (M = 3.76) than among those without such experience (M = 4.16). Descriptively, respondents with direct Greek pension-system experience report lower mean support for the role of private insurers.

However, Levene's test for equality of variances is significant (F = 5.636, p = 0.021), indicating unequal variances across the two groups. Therefore, the appropriate result is the equal variances not assumed row. On that basis, the difference between groups is not statistically significant (t = -1.767, df = 32.485, p = 0.087).

Table 4.8: Independent samples t-test

Test	t	df	p-value	Interpretation
Equal variances not assumed	-1.767	32.485	0.087	Not statistically significant

In examining the impact of prior experience with the Greek pension system on perceptions of the role of private insurers, a non-significant result was found (t = -1.767, p = 0.087). Although respondents with direct experience reported slightly lower mean values (M = 3.76) than those without such experience (M = 4.16), the difference was not statistically significant. The effect size, calculated as Cohen's d using a pooled standard deviation, was 0.51, which falls in the medium range by conventional benchmarks. This indicates that the observed mean difference was not trivially small in magnitude, but that the study was insufficiently powered to detect it reliably at the conventional alpha level. The non-significant result should therefore be interpreted as inconclusive rather than as evidence of no group difference. The descriptive pattern—whereby respondents with direct institutional experience tend toward more cautious assessments of the insurer role—remains analytically relevant and is consistent with the broader finding that familiarity with system constraints tempers optimism about supplementary solutions. This does not change the overall direction of the findings, but it indicates that support for supplementary pension solutions may not be identical across all stakeholder groups, and that a larger sample would be required to test this difference with adequate statistical power.

From a practical perspective, this finding is relevant because it suggests that experience with the Greek pension system may be associated with a more careful or realistic assessment of private insurance solutions, even if the statistical evidence does not support a significant group difference. Respondents with direct experience may be more aware of institutional constraints, implementation barriers, and trust-related challenges that affect the expansion of supplementary pensions. For policymakers and insurers, this indicates that communication and product strategies should not assume uniform stakeholder attitudes. Instead, they should recognise that technically professionally relevant stakeholders may require stronger evidence of regulatory stability, consumer protection, and operational feasibility before fully endorsing a broader role for private insurers.

4.6 Regression Analysis

Two regression models were estimated. The first examines predictors of long-term sustainability perceptions. The second examines predictors of the view that private insurance products are essential to address future adequacy gaps.

4.6.1. Model 1: Predicting perceptions of long-term sustainability

The dependent variable for Model 1 is: "Greece's pension system is currently sustainable in the long term."

The predictors are:

- Greece's pension system is under significant pressure due to the ageing population
- Private insurers can play an important role in supporting Greece's pension system
- Greece needs to reform its tax incentives for private pension savings to increase participation

Table 4.9: Model 1 summary

Model statistic	**Value**
R	0.337
R Square	0.113
Adjusted R Square	0.072
Std. Error of Estimate	0.991
F	2.727
Sig.	0.051

The model explains 11.3% of the variance in sustainability perceptions, with an adjusted R^2 of 0.072. The overall model does not reach statistical significance at the 0.05 level ($F = 2.727$, $p = 0.051$). This indicates that the set of predictors, taken together, provides limited explanatory power for sustainability perceptions in the present sample.

Table 4.10: Model 1 coefficients

Predictor	**B**	**Std. Error**	**Beta**	**t**	**Sig.**
Constant	5.515	1.146	—	4.813	0.000
Ageing pressure	-0.601	0.254	-0.344	-2.367	0.021
Private insurers important	-0.136	0.193	-0.106	-0.704	0.484
Tax reform needed	0.040	0.184	0.037	0.216	0.829

Only ageing pressure is a significant predictor (B = -0.601, p = 0.021). The negative coefficient indicates that stronger recognition of demographic pressure is associated with lower perceptions of long-term sustainability. The other two predictors, support for private insurers and support for tax reform, are not significant.

This result suggests that, within the present sample, perceptions of demographic strain are more closely associated with sustainability judgments than support for private insurers or tax reform. Respondents may therefore distinguish between recognising potential reform tools and believing that the existing pension system is sustainable in the long term. However, this interpretation should be treated with caution, given the limited explanatory power of the model and the fact that the overall model does not reach statistical significance at the 0.05 level.

This finding is consistent with RQ1. It indicates that demographic change is central to perceptions of sustainability constraints. It also suggests that sustainability judgments are broader and more structural than simple confidence in supplementary pension expansion. This is analytically significant because it shows that respondents do not automatically assume private insurance can solve the sustainability problem at the system level, even if they regard it as important.

The near-significance of the overall model (p = 0.051) is itself informative from a practitioner perspective. It does not indicate a failed analysis. Rather, it reflects the multi-dimensional nature of sustainability perceptions in a complex institutional environment. Sustainability judgements in the Greek pension context are shaped by historical experience, fiscal memory, and political uncertainty in ways that a three-predictor model cannot fully capture. Several alternative explanations for the model's limited explanatory power merit consideration. First, sustainability perceptions may be driven primarily by macroeconomic and institutional factors that lie outside the scope of the survey instrument, such as confidence in public administration, experience of pension cuts, or broader political trust. Second, the three predictors may not be sufficiently independent in respondents' mental models; if demographic pressure, insurer importance, and tax reform are perceived as aspects of a single reform problem rather than analytically distinct drivers, their individual coefficients will be attenuated in a multivariate framework. Third, the near-significance of the model ($p = 0.051$) in combination with the small effect size ($f^2 = 0.127$) and the power analysis reported in Chapter 3 suggests that a larger sample may have produced a significant result; the non-significance may partly reflect a power limitation rather than a genuine absence of relationship. For policymakers and insurance-sector decision-makers, this result carries a practical message: no single lever, whether demographic awareness, insurer support, or tax reform, is sufficient on its own to shift sustainability confidence. What is required is coordinated action across multiple institutional dimensions simultaneously. This interpretation is consistent with the broader argument of the dissertation and reinforces the case for a multi-pillar approach grounded in governance, transparency, and long-term policy stability.

4.6.2. Model 2: Private insurance as a Solution to Adequacy Gaps

The dependent variable for Model 2 is: "The introduction of private insurance products will be essential to address future pension adequacy gaps in Greece."

The predictors are:

- Greece's pension system is under significant pressure due to the ageing population
- Private insurers can play an important role in supporting Greece's pension system
- Greece needs to reform its tax incentives for private pension savings to increase participation
- Greece's pension system needs to diversify its sources of retirement income to ensure long-term sustainability

Table 4.11: Model 2 summary

Model statistic	Value
R	0.655
R Square	0.429
Adjusted R Square	0.393
Std. Error of Estimate	0.703
F	11.848
Sig.	0.000

This model is clearly stronger than Model 1. It explains 42.9% of the variance in the dependent variable, with an adjusted R^2 of 0.393, and the model is highly significant overall ($F = 11.848$, $p < 0.001$).

Table 4.12: Model 2 coefficients

Predictor	B	Std. Error	Beta	t	Sig.
Constant	0.425	0.814	—	0.522	0.604
Ageing pressure	0.006	0.200	0.004	0.028	0.978
Private insurers important	0.546	0.151	0.484	3.625	0.001
Tax reform needed	0.069	0.132	0.074	0.523	0.602
Diversification needed	0.237	0.159	0.199	1.495	0.140

Only one predictor is statistically significant at the 0.05 level: Private insurers can play an important role in supporting Greece's pension system ($B = 0.546$, $p = 0.001$).

This represents a statistically robust association within the present sample. Controlling for the other predictors, the strongest determinant of support for private insurance products as a response to future adequacy gaps is whether respondents already perceive private insurers as important actors in the Greek pension context. While intuitive, this finding is analytically relevant because it suggests that support for future private insurance solutions rests less on abstract demographic concern and more on a concrete belief in insurer relevance and capacity.

Although diversification is positively associated with the dependent variable, it is not significant at the 0.05 level in the multivariate model ($p = 0.140$). Tax reform and ageing pressure are also not significant. Once the perceived importance of private insurers is included in the model, the remaining predictors do not explain additional unique variance. The non-significance of tax reform need as a predictor of support for private insurance products carries a substantive message for policymakers that warrants explicit attention. If respondents who strongly favour tax incentives do not systematically show higher support for private insurance products, this suggests that the relationship between fiscal policy levers and market demand is not straightforward. It may indicate that respondents evaluate the desirability of tax reform and the desirability of private insurance provision through largely separate frames of judgement, or that the sample was too homogeneous in its general support for both to allow the relationship to emerge statistically. For policymakers, this null result cautions against the assumption that tax incentives alone will translate into increased consumer uptake of supplementary pension products. Trust, product design, and regulatory quality may be more proximate drivers of demand than fiscal incentives, even when fiscal reform is broadly supported. Similarly, the non-significance of diversification need as an independent predictor, once insurer importance is controlled, suggests that broad support for income diversification does not add explanatory power beyond what respondents' views on insurers already capture. This may reflect construct overlap, or it may indicate that diversification is viewed primarily through the lens of insurer-provided solutions rather than as an independent policy objective.

This model offers strong support for RQ3, because it shows that the perceived importance of insurers is the strongest attitudinal correlate of support for private insurance products as a response to future adequacy problems. It also contributes to RQ2, because it empirically links future adequacy-gap concerns to support for supplementary market-based instruments.

Given the sample size of 68 respondents, the regression models are interpreted as exploratory rather than predictive tools. The objective was not to establish causal relationships or to generate statistically generalisable forecasts, but to identify observable associations within the stakeholder dataset. The models were specified with a limited number of variables in order to avoid overfitting and to preserve interpretative clarity. Results are therefore presented as indicative patterns that support the broader analytical discussion, rather than as definitive statistical conclusions. In line with the applied nature of this dissertation, regression findings are considered in conjunction with descriptive results and institutional context.

4.7 Chapter Summary

This chapter analysed the survey evidence on the sustainability of the Greek pension system, the role of demographic change, and the contribution of private insurers and policy reforms to future retirement provision.

Several main conclusions emerge. First, respondents show low confidence in the current Greek pension system's long-term sustainability and future adequacy. Second, they identify demographic ageing as a major and continuing source of pressure, and this is the only significant individual predictor of sustainability perceptions in Model 1. Third, they show strong support for private insurers as part of a supplementary pension solution, especially where products are simple, transparent, and oriented toward longevity-risk management. Fourth, they support a range of policy and regulatory reforms, especially tax incentives, consumer protection, and diversification of retirement income sources, while expressing limited confidence that current government efforts are sufficient. Fifth, respondents with direct experience of the Greek pension system are somewhat more cautious about insurers' role, although this difference is not statistically significant.

Taken together, the findings suggest that demographic pressure, pension adequacy concerns, and conditional support for private insurers form the central empirical pattern of the study. They indicate that private insurers are seen mainly as complementary actors within a more diversified and better-governed pension structure rather than as a substitute for the public pillar.

The chapter also shows that these findings should be read together rather than as separate empirical observations. Low confidence in sustainability and adequacy is closely connected to the strong perception of demographic pressure, while support for private insurers is clearly conditional on product design, trust, and regulation. In this sense, the results do not point to a simple shift from public provision to private solutions. Instead, they suggest that the main challenge for Greece is how to develop a more coherent pension structure in which supplementary provision can help to address adequacy risks without weakening the central role of the public pillar. This broader pattern is important because it links the statistical findings to the wider institutional and policy questions that are addressed in the following chapter.

The survey instrument also included open-ended questions in Section 6 inviting respondents to elaborate on necessary systemic changes, the evolving role of private insurers, and structural barriers to supplementary pension expansion in Greece. Given the exploratory and supplementary nature of these qualitative responses, and the limited analytical space available within the quantitative framework of this chapter, the substantive content of these responses is addressed in Chapter 5, Section 5.10, where a practitioner-oriented synthesis integrates the qualitative insights alongside the quantitative findings. This approach ensures that the open-ended data contribute meaningfully to the study's conclusions without disrupting the analytical coherence of the quantitative reporting in this chapter.

Chapter 5 DISCUSSION AND RECOMMENDATIONS

This chapter interprets and contextualises the empirical findings presented in Chapter 4 in relation to the dissertation's main research question and subsidiary research questions. Whereas Chapter 4 focused on reporting the results of the survey analysis, the purpose of this chapter is to explain what those findings mean, how they relate to the existing literature, and what implications they carry for pension policy and insurance practice in Greece.

The discussion links the survey findings to the dissertation's central concern, namely the long-term sustainability and adequacy of the Greek pension system and the potential complementary role of private insurers. Overall, the findings suggest that demographic pressure, pension adequacy concerns, and trust-related conditions remain central to the practical viability of a more diversified pension model.

5.1 Summary of Key Findings

The findings from Chapter 4 can be summarised in five broad points.

First, respondents showed low confidence in the long-term sustainability and future adequacy of the Greek pension system. The public pension system was not widely perceived as sufficiently capable of meeting future retirement needs under current conditions. This result is important because it confirms that the study's core problem is not hypothetical. The concern about sustainability and adequacy is present among respondents with relevant professional or sectoral knowledge.

Second, respondents expressed strong agreement that demographic ageing places significant pressure on the Greek pension system, and that this pressure will continue over the long term. This was one of the strongest findings in the dataset and emerged consistently across descriptive, reliability, correlation, and regression analyses.

Third, respondents expressed strong support for a meaningful role for private insurers within the Greek pension landscape. They not only agreed that private insurers can play an important role, but also linked insurer involvement to the reduction of pressure on the public pension system and the closing of future pension adequacy gaps. They also strongly endorsed simple, transparent, and longevity-oriented retirement products.

Fourth, respondents supported a range of policy and regulatory measures that could enable supplementary pensions to develop more effectively, including tax reform, stronger consumer protection, greater integration between public and private pillars, and exploration of cross-border pension arrangements. At the same time, they were less convinced that the Greek government is currently doing enough to support the development of supplementary schemes.

Fifth, the inferential analysis showed a mixed but informative pattern. Demographic pressure significantly predicted perceptions of sustainability in the first regression model, while perceptions of the importance of private insurers significantly predicted support for private insurance products in the second model. By contrast, some anticipated differences between groups, and some policy variables in the regression models, were not statistically significant. Rather than weakening the study, these mixed results help show that pension reform attitudes are structured but not simplistic.

These findings together suggest that respondents do not see the future of Greek pensions as lying in the preservation of the existing public model alone, nor in a simple market replacement of public provision. Instead, they support a more diversified and better-designed supplementary system in which private insurers play a significant but carefully governed role.

5.2 Discussion in Relation to Research Questions

5.2.1. Demographic Change and Pension Sustainability

The findings strongly support the view that demographic change is the most important structural factor reshaping sustainability constraints in the Greek pension system. Respondents overwhelmingly agreed that the system is under pressure due to population ageing and that demographic ageing will continue to strain the system over the next 50 years. Moreover, the regression analysis showed that perceived ageing pressure was the only statistically significant predictor of perceptions of long-term sustainability in Model 1. The regression coefficient for perceived ageing pressure remains statistically significant, indicating its dominant explanatory role in sustainability perceptions.

This finding is highly consistent with the literature reviewed in Chapter 2. The European Commission's 2024 Ageing Report identifies Greece as one of the countries facing intense long-run pension pressure due to adverse population dynamics, including ageing, labour force contraction, and rising dependency ratios (European Commission, 2024). The World Bank (2025) and Eurostat (2023, 2024a) similarly show that Greece faces a pronounced old-age dependency trajectory, low fertility, and long life expectancy, all of which reduce the contributor-to-beneficiary balance central to pay-as-you-go financing. OECD work also reinforces that pension sustainability becomes more difficult when societies age without corresponding increases in working lives, productivity, or diversified retirement income sources (OECD, 2024; OECD, 2024a).

The empirical findings therefore confirm the literature's main diagnosis: the sustainability problem is not simply a matter of technical mismanagement or temporary fiscal imbalance. It is rooted in a structural demographic transformation that is likely to persist over decades. This has two important implications.

The first is that respondents do not appear to believe that the Greek pension system can rely on parametric reform alone. Although Greece has already undergone repeated reform waves, including higher retirement ages, tighter eligibility, contribution recalibration, and administrative consolidation, respondents still expressed doubt that current reforms are enough to guarantee long-term sustainability. This aligns with Kangur et al. (2021), who argue that while Greek pension reforms significantly improved fiscal indicators and reduced fragmentation, they did not eliminate the structural tension between an ageing population and a predominantly PAYG financing model. It also reflects the broader point made by Rotschedl et al. (2024), namely that PAYG systems can address short-term imbalances through parametric adjustments but remain highly exposed to long-term demographic mismatches.

The second implication is that respondents' sustainability concerns seem to be broader than immediate fiscal cost management. Their relatively strong support for the statement that Greece should prioritise pension sustainability over short-term fiscal relief indicates that they view pension sustainability as a strategic, intergenerational issue, not simply an accounting problem. This interpretation fits well with the literature on pension governance, which increasingly stresses that sustainability should not be understood only as public expenditure control but as the long-run capacity of a system to remain both financially viable and socially legitimate (European Commission, 2024; OECD, 2024a).

At the same time, the results also suggest that respondents do not see demographic change as operating in isolation. The significant correlations between demographic pressure and support for tax reform, diversification, and private insurance imply that respondents interpret demographic strain as something that should trigger institutional adaptation. In that sense, ageing is not only seen as a burden; it is also seen as a reason to rethink system design. This is an important nuance. The findings do not merely confirm demographic pessimism. They suggest that respondents understand sustainability as increasingly dependent on a broader multi-pillar strategy.

These findings also reinforce the broader argument that demographic change should not be interpreted as a temporary background factor, but as a structural constraint that reshapes the policy space of the Greek pension system over the long term. In this respect, the survey responses are consistent with the literature reviewed in Chapter 2, which emphasised the significance of rising old-age dependency ratios, low fertility, and increasing longevity for the sustainability of pay-as-you-go pension provision. The empirical evidence presented here suggests that respondents do not expect these pressures to ease through incremental adjustments alone. Instead, demographic ageing appears to be understood as a persistent driver of reform pressure that requires longer-term institutional adaptation. This interpretation is important because it shifts the debate away from short-run fiscal management and toward the more strategic question of how Greece can maintain pension sustainability in a context where the demographic foundation of the traditional system continues to weaken.

5.2.2. Emerging Pension Adequacy Risks in the Greek System

The results indicate that respondents are concerned not only about sustainability, but also about future pension adequacy. In fact, perceptions of adequacy were even more negative than perceptions of sustainability, with the adequacy item receiving one of the lowest mean scores in the survey. The findings show that respondents differentiate between the system's financial viability and its capacity to deliver adequate retirement income.

This distinction is important. A pension system can improve its fiscal sustainability through benefit restraint, stricter eligibility, or lower replacement rates, but these same measures can produce adequacy risks, particularly for lower-income earners, fragmented workers, or those with interrupted contribution histories. The Greek case is especially relevant here because post-crisis pension reforms were heavily oriented toward fiscal consolidation, cost containment, and harmonisation, often at the expense of perceived benefit security and public trust (Kangur et al., 2021; Laliotis et al., 2023).

The survey results are consistent with this interpretation. Respondents showed high agreement that reforms should focus on ensuring adequate income despite demographic pressures, and they also supported the diversification of retirement income sources. At the same time, there was substantial support for the view that private insurance products would be essential to address future pension adequacy gaps. The results reflect a perceived structural gap between public pension sustainability and future adequacy expectations.

Several studies back this up. The OECD (2024a) says funded supplementary pensions matter partly because they can fill adequacy gaps – gaps that appear when PAYG schemes become less generous or hit fiscal limits. The World Bank (2020) has made a similar point for a long time: diversified retirement systems spread risk better across public, occupational, and personal sources. That makes them more resilient. Looking at Greece, Chrysanthopoulou et al. (2023) note that funded occupational mechanisms are still fairly small, but they are becoming more relevant for long-term diversification. Konstantinidou and Koumarianos (2025) add that retirement in Greece will probably become more flexible and more varied. That raises a question: how do you keep adequacy fair across groups with different work histories and different saving capacities?

The results also suggest that respondents interpret adequacy gaps in a forward-looking way. The item on sufficient demand for supplementary pension products in Greece received a lower mean than many other items, which may imply that respondents recognise a tension: they see a future need for supplementary pensions, but they are not yet fully convinced that current market demand is strong enough to close the gap on its own. This is an important insight. It suggests that adequacy gaps may emerge not only because the public system weakens, but also because voluntary supplementary uptake remains limited. In other words, need does not automatically translate into participation.

This interpretation is consistent with recent literature on pension behaviour and long-term saving. Stathopoulos and Vrontos (2025) show that life insurance demand in Greece is affected by macroeconomic conditions and income stability. De Andrés-Sánchez and Puchades (2025) similarly suggest that even when annuitisation has clear welfare value, individuals may not adopt these products if they perceive them as costly, complex, or poor value. Wan et al. (2025) reinforce that demand for retirement-risk management products depends on behavioural factors as much as on actuarial logic. Thus, the adequacy problem is not only institutional and fiscal. It is also behavioural and market-dependent.

For this dissertation, the main implication is that adequacy gaps are perceived as a likely future problem and that respondents see supplementary insurance products as part of the answer. However, the findings also imply that these products will only play a meaningful role if issues of access, trust, affordability, and consumer understanding are addressed. Adequacy, therefore, cannot be treated as something the private sector will solve automatically. It remains a public-policy challenge even when private provision becomes more relevant.

An important implication of these findings is that sustainability and adequacy should not be treated as interchangeable concepts in pension reform. A system may achieve a degree of fiscal stabilisation while still generating growing concerns about the adequacy of future retirement income. The survey results point clearly in this direction. While respondents expressed scepticism about the long-term sustainability of the Greek pension system, they were even less confident that the current pay-as-you-go structure would be adequate to meet the future needs of retirees. This distinction matters because it suggests that reform success cannot be judged solely by expenditure control or fiscal indicators. From a policy and managerial perspective, the results imply that future pension debates in

Greece must pay closer attention to the risk that reforms may improve financial discipline while leaving future retirees exposed to income insecurity, especially in the context of longer life expectancy, fragmented careers, and limited private saving capacity.

5.2.3. The Strategic Role of Private Insurers in Pension Provision

This is the research question most strongly supported by the empirical evidence. Across the survey, respondents consistently expressed support for the role of private insurers in Greece's evolving pension system. The private insurance role scale showed very high reliability, and the strongest correlations in the analysis were between the items capturing insurer importance, insurers' essential role in reducing public pressure, and the importance of private insurance products in addressing adequacy gaps. In addition, the second regression model showed that the belief that private insurers can play an important role was the strongest predictor of support for private insurance products as a future adequacy solution.

The results therefore suggest that respondents do not view private insurers as marginal actors or optional add-ons. Rather, they see them as potentially significant participants in a broader retirement-income architecture. However, the support expressed is not generic. The descriptive findings indicate that respondents favour specific insurer capabilities and product characteristics.

The clearest result in this regard is the very high support for simple and transparent pension products. This is one of the strongest mean scores in the dataset. The importance of this finding should not be underestimated. It suggests that respondents see product design as central to the credibility and usefulness of supplementary pensions. In a country such as Greece, where trust in long-term institutional promises has been weakened by repeated reforms, crisis-era welfare adjustments, and economic uncertainty, product complexity can be a major barrier to adoption. The literature strongly supports this interpretation. The post-crisis Greek context has been shaped by uncertainty and reform fatigue, which can reduce willingness to commit to long-term financial arrangements (Laliotis et al., 2023). At the same time, research on annuity and retirement products consistently finds that complexity reduces uptake and weakens perceived value (De Andrés-Sánchez & Puchades, 2025; Wan et al., 2025).

The second key capability concerns longevity-risk management. Respondents strongly supported the idea that insurers should provide products addressing longevity risk and that annuities can reduce the risk of outliving retirement savings. This is consistent with the core insurance function of pooling long-term risks that individuals struggle to manage on their own. Hanbali (2024) argues that annuity structures and longevity risk-sharing mechanisms remain among the most powerful tools for stabilising income in old age, even if their attractiveness to consumers depends heavily on product framing and design. In that sense, the results suggest that respondents see insurers' value less in replacing public pensions and more in providing specialist mechanisms that the public pillar cannot efficiently deliver on its own.

A third capability implied by the findings is institutional investment and long-horizon asset management. Although not directly measured as a separate survey item, this theme emerges indirectly from respondents' support for diversification and the relevance of insurers in supplementary provision. The literature indicates that insurers and other long-term institutional investors can contribute to funded pension systems through asset-liability matching, diversified investment management, and decumulation design (OECD, 2024a; Bank of Greece, 2025a). In the Greek context, where funded pension pillars remain relatively small, the ability of private insurers to operate as credible long-term financial institutions may become more important over time.

At the same time, the findings caution against overstating the role of insurers. Respondents with direct experience of the Greek pension system appear somewhat more cautious, even though the difference is not statistically strong. This suggests that insurer capability depends not only on technical expertise, but also on whether products are trusted, accessible, and well governed in the Greek context.

The findings therefore suggest that the most relevant insurer capabilities for Greece are product simplicity and transparency, longevity-risk pooling and annuity design, credible long-term saving and decumulation mechanisms, and the ability to operate within a strong governance and consumer-protection framework.

This is consistent with the literature reviewed in Chapter 2 and supports the dissertation's argument that private insurers can play a strategic role in a multi-pillar system, but only under conditions that make their products understandable, fair, and socially credible.

The findings suggest that support for private insurers is not unconditional. Rather than endorsing a broad expansion of private pension provision in abstract terms, respondents appear to link the legitimacy of insurers to concrete capabilities and product features. In particular, strong approval of simple and transparent pension products, together with positive assessments of annuities and longevity-risk solutions, indicates that insurers are viewed as valuable where they contribute to clarity, effective risk management, and stable retirement income. This interpretation corresponds with the arguments developed in Chapter 2, which emphasised that insurers can play a meaningful role as providers of funded retirement products, long-term investors, and managers of longevity-related risks, provided that regulatory design supports trust and consumer confidence. Overall, the results point to private insurers functioning as complements to public pension provision in Greece, especially in addressing adequacy gaps, rather than as substitutes for the public pillar.

5.2.4. Policy Pathways for Expanding Supplementary Pensions

The findings suggest substantial support for a reform agenda aimed at expanding supplementary pensions, but they also show that respondents do not view policy reform as a simple, single-dimensional matter. Support was high for tax reform, stronger consumer protection, integration between public and private systems, auto-enrolment, and stronger roles for EU and EIOPA-level governance. At the same time, respondents did not believe that the Greek government is currently doing enough to support supplementary pension development. This implies that there is broad support for reform in principle but limited confidence in the present policy environment.

This pattern aligns with literature. EIOPA (2024) and the European Court of Auditors (2025) both note that supplementary and personal pension expansion in Europe has been limited by fragmented national systems, inconsistent tax treatment, weak incentives, and low provider engagement in cross-border products such as PEPP. The Greek case seems to reflect many of these broader obstacles. Respondents appear to believe that supplementary pension growth requires more than individual willingness to save. It also depends on institutional incentives, credible rules, and stronger frameworks for consumer protection.

The high level of support for tax incentives reflects the view that supplementary pension growth depends on fiscal encouragement. This is consistent with both European and international evidence. Funded pensions often grow where tax and contribution incentives make long-term saving more attractive, especially where voluntary participation would otherwise remain weak (OECD, 2024a). The Greek case is especially relevant because households' capacity to save remains uneven after the crisis, and voluntary supplementary products may remain concentrated among higher-income groups unless participation is supported more actively.

Support for consumer protection is equally significant. This finding suggests that respondents recognise the risks of mistrust, mis-selling, and complexity in long-term financial products. In a context where respondents also strongly value simple and transparent products, stronger consumer protection seems to function as a trust-building mechanism, not merely as a compliance requirement. This interpretation fits the literature on trust and pension participation. Low trust can undermine uptake even when products are financially rational, particularly in environments shaped by policy reversals and economic instability (Laliotis et al., 2023; De Andrés-Sánchez & Puchades, 2025).

The relatively low reliability of the policy-related items scale is also informative. It indicates that respondents do not necessarily treat tax incentives, auto-enrolment, integration, and consumer protection as aspects of a single reform package. Rather, they evaluate them separately. This suggests that pension reform in Greece is likely to require a differentiated policy strategy. For example, fiscal incentives may be relevant for participation, while consumer protection may matter more for trust, and integration may matter more for long-term system coherence. The low alpha, therefore, should not be seen simply as a methodological weakness. It reflects the practical reality that policy measures work through different channels and are likely to be judged on different criteria.

Finally, support for EU/EIOPA involvement and for exploring PEPP-related and cross-border solutions suggests that respondents do not see the Greek pension challenge as entirely national in solution terms. This does not mean they believe EU-level frameworks are sufficient on their own. Rather, it suggests that they value supranational governance as a support for credibility, fairness, and market development. This aligns with the literature showing that national pension systems increasingly operate within wider regulatory and supervisory environments, even if actual market uptake remains nationally uneven (EIOPA, 2024; Guardiancich & Natali, 2011).

Overall, the answer to RQ4 is that supplementary pensions in Greece are most likely to expand under a combined policy framework involving tax reform, stronger consumer protection, clearer public-private integration, and credible supervisory support. However, the findings also imply that policy reform must be carefully designed because respondents do not see all measures as interchangeable or equally coherent.

The policy-related findings further suggest that respondents favour an enabling framework for supplementary pension development rather than a narrow market-led expansion. Support for tax incentives, stronger consumer protection, greater public-private integration, and policy instruments such as auto-enrolment indicates that respondents do not view supplementary pensions as self-sustaining products that will expand without institutional support. Instead, the findings point to a governance-oriented interpretation in which participation, fairness, and trust depend on the quality of the surrounding policy framework. This is especially significant in the Greek context, where low confidence in long-term financial commitments may constrain demand even when retirement risks are widely recognised. The results therefore support the argument that regulatory and policy reform must not only encourage supplementary pension uptake, but also strengthen the legitimacy and transparency of the system if private pension expansion is to be socially and politically sustainable.

These findings also suggest that policy reform should not be approached as a set of separate measures that operate independently from one another. Tax incentives may help to increase participation, but their effect is likely to remain limited if households do not trust the products offered or if supplementary pension saving continues to be perceived as complex and unclear. In a similar way, auto-enrolment may support broader participation, but without strong consumer protection and transparent product design it may not produce lasting confidence. Greater integration between the public and private pillars is therefore relevant not only for institutional coordination, but also for public legitimacy. In the Greek context, this means that policy and regulatory reform should be developed in stages: first by strengthening trust and transparency, second by improving participation incentives, and third by embedding supplementary pensions more firmly within a coherent multi-pillar framework. This is consistent with the wider finding of this thesis that pension sustainability cannot be strengthened through market expansion alone, but requires coordination between policymakers, regulators, and private providers.

This also means that the success of supplementary pension expansion should not be judged only by the formal availability of products or by the existence of new regulatory measures. A broader market would have limited value if participation remained concentrated among higher-income groups, while large parts of the population continued to rely almost entirely on a pressured public system. For this reason, policy pathways should also be evaluated in terms of accessibility, fairness, and practical feasibility for households, rather than only in terms of institutional reform on paper.

Table 5.1: Mapping of Chapter 5 Sections to Research Questions

Section	Research Question (RQ)	Key Findings (Chapter 4)	Discussion (Chapter 5)
Demographic Pressure	RQ1	High means (4.31-4.34) for demographic ageing as a pressure factor.	Demographic change is a primary constraint on the sustainability of Greece's pension system.
Pension Adequacy Gaps	RQ2	Low means for adequacy (2.28) and sustainability (2.53).	Emerging gaps from pension reforms due to demographic challenges.
Role of Private Insurers	RQ3	Strong support for insurers' role (4.01-4.43, alpha = 0.870).	Insurers can play a strategic role in ensuring long-term adequacy through products like annuities.
Policy Measures	RQ4	High support for tax reform (4.24), auto-enrolment (3.93), and integration (4.01).	Policy levers such as tax reform, auto-enrolment, and stronger consumer protection are critical for strengthening supplementary pensions.

5.3 Comparison of Findings with Existing Literature

In this section, we compare the key findings of this study with the existing body of literature on pension sustainability, adequacy, and demographic pressures, focusing particularly on the role of private insurers and policy reforms. By examining the congruence and divergence between the current research and previous studies, we can better understand the significance of the findings and their implications for policy.

Demographic Pressures on Pension Sustainability (RQ1)

The findings of this research align with a substantial body of literature that highlights ageing populations as a major challenge to pension system sustainability. As identified in this research, the ageing population in Greece places considerable strain on the pay-as-you-go (PAYG) system, which is dependent on a large working-age population to fund pension payments for retirees.

Research by **Börsch-Supan and Wilke (2004)**, and **Börsch-Supan et al. (2015)** confirms that demographic shifts, particularly the ageing population, create significant challenges for the **sustainability of public pension systems** in Europe. Similarly, **Myles (2002)** and **Feldstein (2005)** argue that as the proportion of retirees increases, systems reliant on current workers' contributions (like the PAYG system) face funding gaps, which can jeopardize their long-term sustainability.

The findings in this study, specifically the high mean scores for ageing pressures (M = 4.31–4.34) and the regression analysis showing that ageing pressures negatively affect sustainability, confirm the findings of these scholars. The negative regression coefficient ($B = -0.601$, $p = 0.021$) highlights the strong predictive relationship between ageing and sustainability, which is consistent with the demographic challenges identified in the literature.

However, this dissertation extends existing research by highlighting policy interventions and private sector involvement as necessary components for addressing these demographic pressures. In contrast to studies that focus primarily on public pension reforms, this research emphasizes the importance of integrating private insurance products into the pension system to manage long-term risks.

What is particularly important in the Greek case is that demographic pressure is not perceived as a temporary policy difficulty, but as a structural condition that continues even after repeated reform efforts. This makes the present findings consistent with the literature not only at a general European level, but also in a more specific Greek context where fiscal consolidation has improved some indicators without removing the underlying ageing problem. In this sense, the study supports the argument that demographic pressure should be understood less as an external variable and more as a core organising constraint of pension reform itself. The findings therefore reinforce the view that sustainability debates in Greece cannot be reduced to short-term expenditure control, because the deeper issue concerns the changing balance between contributors and beneficiaries over the long term.

Pension Adequacy and Emerging Gaps Post-Reforms (RQ2)

The study's findings regarding pension adequacy (mean = 2.28) confirm the growing concern about the adequacy of pension systems in the face of demographic changes. Respondents expressed concern about future pension income, reflecting the adequacy gaps identified in the literature.

OECD (2015) and Börsch-Supan et al. (2014) argue that pension reforms, particularly those focused on sustainability (e.g., raising retirement ages or reducing benefits), often inadvertently lead to lower replacement rates, thus exacerbating adequacy gaps. Similarly, Vittas (2000) discusses how adequacy gaps widen when public pension systems are reformed without integrating complementary private savings mechanisms.

The investigation confirms the literature's findings on the emerging gaps in pension adequacy after recent reforms. The strong correlation ($r = 0.777$, $p < 0.01$) between sustainability and adequacy, and the respondents' concerns about future income shortfalls, further corroborate the literature's assertion that reforms often create new challenges in pension adequacy. The current study contributes to this understanding by emphasizing the importance of private insurers in addressing these gaps through longevity risk management products (e.g., annuities), which have received strong support from stakeholders (mean = 4.43).

An important implication of this result is that adequacy concerns appear to be more than a secondary consequence of sustainability reform. Rather, the findings suggest that adequacy has become a central issue in its own right. This is especially relevant in Greece, where repeated pension adjustments may have improved fiscal discipline, but may also have increased uncertainty about the long-term capacity of the system to provide sufficient retirement income. In that respect, the present findings are consistent with the literature that warns against treating sustainability and adequacy as separable policy goals. The Greek case instead illustrates that reforms aimed at stabilising the system may simultaneously intensify concerns about the quality of retirement outcomes, particularly for future pensioners who will rely on a more constrained public system.

The Role of Private Insurers in Pension Sustainability (RQ3)

The role of private insurers in supporting pension sustainability was another focal point of this research. Respondents expressed relatively strong support for the view that private insurers can help address longevity risk and contribute to pension adequacy, particularly through annuities and related retirement products.

The literature on private insurance in pension systems generally emphasises the importance of risk diversification and longevity-risk management. Dushi and Webb (2004) argue that products such as annuities can reduce the risk of individuals outliving their savings. Similarly, Munnell and Soto (2007) suggest that private-sector involvement may become more important where public pension systems face growing financial pressure.

The findings of the present study are broadly consistent with this literature. The relatively high mean scores (4.01–4.43) for the effectiveness of private insurers, together with the positive regression result ($B = 0.546$, $p = 0.001$), indicate that many stakeholders see private insurance products as potentially important in supporting pension sustainability and addressing adequacy pressures. This suggests that insurers are viewed not only as supplementary actors, but as increasingly relevant components within a broader multi-pillar pension framework.

At the same time, the study adds to the discussion by highlighting continued concerns about consumer trust and understanding. This suggests that the contribution of private insurers depends not only on product availability, but also on transparency, communication, and financial literacy if broader engagement with private pension products is to develop.

Policy Measures and the Need for Reform (RQ4)

The study shows clear support among stakeholders for a number of policy measures aimed at strengthening pension sustainability. In particular, tax reform, auto-enrolment, and closer integration between public and private pension arrangements received strong support.

This is broadly consistent with the existing literature. Feldstein (2005) and the OECD (2017) both stress the importance of tax incentives and auto-enrolment in encouraging participation in private pension saving. OECD evidence also points to the experience of countries such as the United Kingdom and New Zealand, where auto-enrolment contributed to higher levels of retirement saving.

The results of the present study point in a similar direction. Support for tax reform recorded a mean score of 4.24, auto-enrolment 3.93, and greater public-private integration 4.01. These results are in line with the wider literature, which treats such measures as important for expanding supplementary pension provision. At the same time, the findings also suggest a more cautious view of the current policy environment.

Respondents gave a much lower mean score of 2.63 to the view that government efforts have so far been sufficient. This implies that even where support for reform is strong in principle, its successful implementation still depends on a more credible and effective regulatory framework.

More broadly, the study supports much of the existing literature on pension sustainability, pension adequacy, and the role of private insurers. The results confirm that demographic pressure, especially population ageing, remains a central challenge for pension-system sustainability, which is consistent with Börsch-Supan et al. (2004) and Feldstein (2005). In a similar way, concerns about pension adequacy and the emergence of post-reform gaps reflect arguments already made by the OECD (2015) and Vittas (2000).

At the same time, the study adds a further point to the discussion by underlining the role of private insurers in managing longevity risk and supporting pension adequacy. This aspect is sometimes less visible in studies that focus mainly on public pension reform. The policy implications that emerge here, especially in relation to tax reform and auto-enrolment, are broadly in line with OECD work, but they also place stronger emphasis on consumer protection and financial literacy. These areas appear particularly important in the Greek context and remain less fully developed in parts of the existing literature.

This also helps explain why the policy-related findings should not be interpreted as support for a simple expansion of private provision. Instead, the evidence points to a coordinated reform logic in which tax incentives, consumer protection, auto-enrolment, and greater institutional integration are understood as mutually reinforcing measures. This is broadly in line with the comparative literature, but the present study gives this argument a more applied emphasis by showing that stakeholders do not only support reform instruments individually; they also appear to recognise the need for a governance framework within which these measures can operate effectively. In the Greek context, this is especially important because weak implementation or low trust could undermine otherwise promising policy tools.

Overall, the comparison with the existing literature shows that the findings of this analysis are not isolated or contradictory, but broadly embedded within established debates on pension sustainability, adequacy, and multi-pillar reform. At the same time, the study contributes a more applied and context-specific perspective by linking these debates to stakeholder perceptions in Greece. This is important because it moves the discussion beyond abstract reform principles and toward the practical conditions under which supplementary pension expansion may or may not become feasible. In this respect, the contribution of the study lies not only in confirming known pressures, but also in clarifying how these pressures are interpreted by actors who are directly relevant to pension policy and insurance practice.

5.4 Theoretical Framing of Pension Diversification and Governance

The findings of this dissertation can also be interpreted within a broader conceptual understanding of pension system design and risk allocation. Although the analysis has focused primarily on the Greek case and its institutional context, the results reflect more general dynamics that are discussed in the literature on multi-pillar pension systems and governance.

Public pay-as-you-go pension systems are built on intergenerational risk-sharing. Their sustainability depends largely on the balance between contributors and beneficiaries. When demographic conditions change, as is currently the case in Greece, this balance becomes more difficult to maintain. Lower fertility rates and increasing life expectancy gradually increase the financial pressure on contribution-based systems. In such a setting, policy responses often involve parametric adjustments, including retirement age changes, contribution rate modifications, or benefit recalibration. However, these measures mainly redistribute pressure within the public pillar rather than fundamentally diversifying risk.

Multi-pillar pension systems aim to address this structural vulnerability by combining different financing mechanisms. Funded supplementary pensions introduce capital accumulation and investment-based elements into retirement income provision. This does not remove uncertainty, but it changes the nature of risk exposure. Demographic risk is partially complemented by market and governance risk. In principle, this diversification can enhance systemic resilience, provided that the funded pillar is well regulated and socially legitimate.

The empirical findings of this study suggest that support for a stronger role of private insurers in Greece is conditional. Stakeholders do not perceive private pension provision as a substitute for the public system, but rather as a potential complement under clearly defined regulatory and governance conditions. This aligns with the broader literature, which emphasises that institutional trust, transparency, and consumer protection are central to the credibility of funded pension arrangements. In this sense, pension diversification is not only a financial strategy but also a governance issue.

The Greek case also shows that the move towards a more balanced multi-pillar structure is gradual and shaped by earlier institutional choices. Existing PAYG obligations still affect fiscal realities, while newer funded elements, such as defined-contribution auxiliary schemes, develop over time. During this transition, coordination between public and private actors is especially important. Without clear regulation, effective communication, and aligned incentives, diversification may remain limited or uneven.

Taken together, the findings of this dissertation support a gradual and complementary approach to pension reform. Diversification through supplementary funded provision can contribute to retirement income stability, but only if it is embedded in a framework that protects adequacy, transparency, and public trust. The theoretical implication is therefore not that funded solutions replace public pensions, but that their contribution depends on governance quality and institutional credibility within the wider pension system.

This also shows that the role of private insurers cannot be understood in isolation from the broader institutional environment. The effectiveness of funded supplementary provision depends on the interaction between demographic trends, fiscal capacity, regulatory design, and public confidence. In this sense, the Greek case shows that pension sustainability is shaped not only by financial parameters, but also by governance structures and credibility over time. The study therefore supports the view that pension diversification is ultimately an issue of institutional coordination rather than only a technical reform option.

5.5 Broader Implications of the Findings

The findings carry implications at three levels: theoretical, policy, and managerial.

At the **theoretical level**, the study supports the argument that pension-system analysis should move beyond purely fiscal or state-centric models. The Greek pension question is not only about whether the public system can remain solvent; it is also about how different pillars of retirement provision can interact under conditions of ageing, trust deficits, and market constraints. The results support a multi-pillar perspective, but not a simplistic one. Private insurers are seen as relevant, yet their role is conditional on institutional design and consumer trust.

At the **policy level**, the findings suggest that reform debates in Greece should not frame the issue as a binary choice between public pensions and privatisation. Respondents appear to support a mixed architecture in which the public system remains foundational, while supplementary funded arrangements become more important in addressing adequacy and risk diversification. This implies that policymakers should focus less on ideological opposition between pillars and more on the design conditions under which supplementary provision can become socially useful and broadly trusted.

At the managerial level, the findings suggest that insurers operating in Greece, or in similar settings, should pay more attention to clarity, simplicity, fairness, and the slow process of building trust over time. The results do not support an approach that relies mainly on product proliferation or technical sophistication by itself. What seems to matter more is whether insurers can show clear value, protect consumers in practice, and position their products in a way that is consistent with broader policy concerns around adequacy and sustainable retirement security.

The findings also have broader implications for how pension reform in Greece is understood. They suggest that pension sustainability should not be treated only as a fiscal issue, but as a wider institutional challenge involving adequacy, trust, participation, and governance. In this context, private insurers are more likely to be accepted as complementary actors when their products are transparent, understandable, and aligned with broader retirement-security goals.

There are also implications for governance. The study suggests that pension reform cannot be understood only as a matter for the state, nor only as a matter for the private market. The more realistic picture is one of interdependence between policymakers, regulators, and providers. Public authorities shape the incentives and legal framework, regulators shape trust through oversight and consumer protection, and insurers shape practical outcomes through product design and communication. This means that pension reform in Greece is likely to be more effective when these actors are treated as part of the same governance structure rather than as separate spheres with unrelated responsibilities.

Finally, the findings suggest that the Greek case has relevance beyond the national setting. While the institutional details are specific to Greece, the underlying tensions identified in this dissertation are common to many ageing societies: demographic pressure on public pension systems, concern about future adequacy, limited trust in long-term financial arrangements, and uncertainty about how far funded supplementary provision can expand in a socially acceptable way. For that reason, the broader implication of this study is not only that Greece needs a more coherent multi-pillar approach, but also that pension reform in ageing societies generally requires more attention to trust, governance, and the practical conditions of household participation.

The findings also have broader implications for the role of private insurers in ageing societies. In the literature, private insurers are often discussed mainly in technical terms, for example as providers of annuities, funded savings products, or longevity-risk solutions. The present study suggests that this is only part of the picture. In practice, their relevance depends not only on actuarial or financial capacity, but also on whether they can operate within a framework that is publicly credible and understandable to consumers. In this respect, the Greek case indicates that insurers are more likely to be accepted as complementary pension actors when they are associated with transparency, product simplicity, and fair treatment, rather than with complexity or aggressive market expansion.

5.6 Limitations of the Findings

The findings should be interpreted with appropriate caution. First, the sample size is modest. Although 68 responses are acceptable for an exploratory DBA study, they do not support broad statistical generalisation to all stakeholders in Greece. Second, the sample is professionally relevant but uneven, with a relatively strong representation of insurance-related respondents. Third, the survey captures perceptions rather than observed behaviour. This means that support for private insurers or supplementary reform does not automatically imply actual market uptake or policy feasibility. Fourth, some scales, especially policy-related items, showed lower internal consistency, suggesting that not all grouped items functioned as unified constructs. Beyond these design-level constraints, a post-study reflection on what the evidence can and cannot establish is warranted at doctoral level. The finding that tax reform need was not a significant predictor of support for private insurance products means that the recommendations in Section 5.7 regarding fiscal incentives rest primarily on descriptive attitudinal data rather than on demonstrated predictive relationships. Policymakers should read the recommendation for tax reform as reflecting broad stakeholder preference rather than as evidence of a causal pathway from tax incentives to market expansion. Similarly, the finding that demographic pressure was the only significant predictor in Model 1, while insurer importance was the only significant predictor in Model 2, defines the evidential boundary of what this study can claim: the two models together suggest that ageing perception drives sustainability concern, and that belief in insurers' importance drives support for their role, but the study cannot establish that improving either perception will produce the other, nor that both together are sufficient to generate the institutional change that effective supplementary pension development would require.

In addition, the cross-sectional design of the study imposes further limitations. The data were collected at one point in time and therefore reflect stakeholder perceptions within a specific institutional and policy context. As a result, the findings cannot establish causal relationships between demographic perceptions, policy preferences, and support for private insurers. The statistical associations identified in Chapter 4 are informative, but they should be interpreted as indicative rather than causal.

A further limitation concerns statistical power. Given the modest sample size, some inferential tests may have had limited ability to detect weaker relationships or subgroup differences. This is relevant in light of the non-significant t-test result and the limited explanatory strength of parts of the regression analysis. While these findings still provide useful descriptive and exploratory insight, they do not justify strong inferential claims about the wider stakeholder population in Greece.

A post-hoc power assessment reinforces this point with analytical precision. For the independent samples t-test comparing respondents with and without prior Greek pension experience ($n_1 = 25$, $n_2 = 43$), the observed

Cohen's d was 0.51, indicating a medium effect size. At this effect size with the achieved sample allocation, the estimated statistical power was approximately 0.40–0.45, substantially below the conventional threshold of 0.80. This means the study had a meaningful probability of failing to detect a real group difference even where one existed. The result should therefore be interpreted as inconclusive rather than as evidence that no difference exists between the two groups. For the regression models, the minimum detectable effect size at adequate power ($f^2 \geq 0.12$) with $N = 68$ and three predictors corresponds to an R^2 of approximately 0.107. Model 1's obtained R^2 of 0.113 is close to this threshold, confirming that the model was operating near the boundary of what the sample could reliably detect. These power limitations do not invalidate the findings but qualify the confidence with which the non-significant results can be interpreted. They are addressed in the interpretation of findings in Chapter 4 and in the limitations section of Chapter 5.

Multicollinearity among the regression predictors was assessed through examination of the correlation matrix prior to model estimation. The correlations among the predictor variables in both models were moderate and below the threshold typically associated with problematic multicollinearity ($r < 0.70$ for all predictor pairs). As a further check, variance inflation factors (VIF) were examined for both regression models. All VIF values were below 2.0, well within the commonly accepted threshold of 10.0 and the more conservative threshold of 5.0, indicating that multicollinearity did not pose a substantive threat to the stability or interpretability of the regression coefficients reported in Chapter 4.

The composition of the sample also affects interpretation. Although the respondents were selected for their professional relevance to the pension and insurance field, access to expert participants in the Greek context was constrained. This means that the achieved sample may reflect a degree of response bias, particularly if individuals with stronger professional interest in pension reform or private insurance were more likely to participate. The findings should therefore be understood as reflecting informed stakeholder views rather than a representative cross-section of all potentially relevant groups.

Another limitation lies in the use of self-reported survey responses. Such data are valuable for examining attitudes, priorities, and perceived barriers, but they are also vulnerable to issues such as response framing, selective interpretation of questions, and socially desirable answering. In a topic such as pension reform, where views may be shaped by institutional position, professional affiliation, or policy expectations, survey responses may capture normative preferences as much as strictly analytical judgments.

Finally, the study remains limited in scope to the Greek case and to a policy-oriented examination of stakeholder perceptions regarding supplementary pension provision. This focus is appropriate for the objectives of the dissertation, but it means that the results should not be transferred mechanically to other pension systems with different institutional, regulatory, or market characteristics. The contribution of the study lies less in universal generalisation than in offering a structured and practice-relevant account of how key stakeholders perceive the sustainability challenges of the Greek pension system and the possible complementary role of private insurers within it.

These limitations do not invalidate the findings, but they do shape how they should be interpreted. The study is best understood as providing a structured and policy-relevant account of stakeholder perceptions, not a final causal model of pension reform outcomes.

A further limitation concerns the gap between stakeholder perception and institutional implementation. The study captures how informed respondents assess sustainability pressures, adequacy risks, and the possible role of private insurers, but it does not test whether these preferences would translate into actual reform outcomes under Greek political and regulatory conditions. This is important because policy support in principle does not necessarily imply implementation capacity in practice. In the Greek context, institutional complexity, administrative constraints, and public distrust may affect the practical viability of supplementary pension reform in ways that are not fully captured by survey-based perception data.

There is also a limitation related to the level of analysis. The study focuses on professionally relevant stakeholders rather than on households, pension beneficiaries, or the general public. This is appropriate in light of the dissertation's applied and policy-oriented objective, but it also means that the findings should not be read as direct evidence of mass public attitudes toward supplementary pension products. Stakeholder views are valuable because they reflect institutional knowledge and sector-specific experience, yet they may differ from the views of ordinary citizens, especially those with lower income, lower financial literacy, or weaker trust in long-term financial arrangements.

In addition, the study does not directly examine actual product performance, long-term return outcomes, or the actuarial pricing of retirement products offered by private insurers. As a result, the analysis can identify support for the role of private insurers and for instruments such as annuities or supplementary pension products, but it cannot determine whether specific products currently available in the Greek or wider European market would deliver adequate value under real market conditions. This means that the study is better understood as a policy and stakeholder analysis than as a technical evaluation of pension product efficiency.

Finally, caution is also needed in interpreting the broader relevance of the findings over time. Pension systems are shaped by long-term demographic trends, but stakeholder views may still shift relatively quickly in response to economic shocks, regulatory change, inflation, or political developments. The present results therefore provide a structured account of perceptions at the time of data collection, rather than a fixed or permanent view of the Greek pension debate. This reinforces the importance of interpreting the findings as time-specific, exploratory, and policy-relevant rather than as definitive evidence of stable long-term preferences.

5.7 Policy Recommendations

Recommendations for Policymakers: These actions are critical for creating the regulatory framework, fiscal environment, and institutional support necessary for enhancing the sustainability and adequacy of Greece's pension system.

1. **Prioritize Tax Reform for Private Pension Savings (Mean = 4.24)**

    - **Action**: Introduce enhanced tax incentives for private pensions to incentivize long-term savings and reduce reliance on the PAYG system.
    - **Priority Level**: High
    - **Timeline**: 12–18 months
    - **Metrics**: Track participation rates (target: 20% increase in 5 years).

2. **Implement Auto-Enrolment for Supplementary Pension Schemes (Mean = 3.93)**

    - **Action**: Introduce mandatory auto-enrolment for new employees in supplementary pension schemes, with an opt-out option.
    - **Priority Level**: Medium-High
    - **Timeline**: 12–24 months
    - **Metrics**: Track enrolment rates (target: 50% participation within 2 years).

3. **Strengthen Consumer Protection Laws (Mean = 4.25)**

- **Action**: Introduce stronger regulations to ensure transparency and fairness in private pension products.
- **Priority Level**: High
- **Timeline**: 6–12 months
- **Metrics**: Measure consumer trust and satisfaction (target: 80% satisfaction within 5 years).

4. **Increase Integration Between Public and Private Pension Systems (Mean = 4.01)**
   - **Action**: Develop mechanisms for integrating private pension contributions with the public system, ensuring complementary rather than competing systems.
   - **Priority Level**: Medium
   - **Timeline**: 2–3 years
   - **Metrics**: Track combined participation in both systems (target: 25% increase by 2027).

5. **Strengthen International Cooperation for Cross-Border Pension Solutions (Mean = 4.09)**
   - **Action**: Enhance Greece's engagement with European institutions (e.g., EU, EIOPA) to promote cross-border pension solutions like the Pan-European Personal Pension Product (PEPP).
   - **Priority Level**: Medium
   - **Timeline**: 12 months
   - **Metrics**: Track PEPP uptake (target: 10% increase in 3 years).

Recommendations for Insurers: Private insurers play a crucial role in offering products, managing risks, and ensuring the long-term adequacy of retirement income. These actions are key to building sustainable, transparent, and consumer-friendly pension solutions.

1. **Design Simple and Transparent Pension Products (Mean = 4.43)**

    - **Action**: Insurers should focus on creating clear, easy-to-understand pension products with transparent fees and benefits.
    - **Why**: Simplified products will build trust and make it easier for consumers to engage with private pensions.
    - **Priority Level**: High
    - **Timeline**: 6–12 months to begin product redesign.
    - **Metrics**: Measure consumer understanding and satisfaction with new products (target: 80% satisfaction within 2 years).

2. **Focus on Longevity Risk Management (Mean = 4.01)**

    - **Action**: Insurers should prioritize the development of annuities and other products that help address longevity risk and the risk of outliving retirement savings.
    - **Why**: Given Greece's ageing population, the need for longevity-risk solutions is paramount.
    - **Priority Level**: High
    - **Timeline**: 12–18 months to design and launch relevant products.
    - **Metrics**: Track the uptake of longevity-focused products (target: 15% increase in sales within 2 years).

3. **Ensure Financial Literacy and Consumer Education (Related to RQ3)**

- **Action**: Insurers should invest in educational campaigns that help consumers understand the value of private pensions and how to choose the right products for their needs.
- **Why**: Many consumers are hesitant to engage with pensions due to lack of understanding and trust.
- **Priority Level**: Medium
- **Timeline**: 12–24 months for the rollout of financial education campaigns.
- **Metrics**: Measure the number of individuals attending educational workshops and their confidence in pension products (target: 50% increase in financial literacy rates).

Table 5.2 summarises the main policy measures emerging from the findings and ranks them according to stakeholder support, practical relevance, estimated implementation cost, and indicative timeframe.

Table 5.2: Prioritised Policy Measures for Supplementary Pensions in Greece

Rank	Policy Measure	Mean Support (1-5)	Key Evidence and Rationale	Estimated Cost	Indicative Timeframe
1	Tax incentives for private pension savings	4.24	Strong descriptive support; positively correlated with support for private insurers ($r = 0.537$, $p < 0.01$) and diversification need ($r = 0.571$, $p < 0.01$), suggesting relevance for participation and system diversification.	Medium	12-18 months
2	Stronger consumer protection laws	4.25	Highest policy-related mean score; also consistent with the finding that respondents do not believe the government is currently doing enough to support supplementary pensions ($M = 2.63$), indicating a trust and governance gap.	Low	6-12 months
3	Auto-enrolment in supplementary schemes	3.93	Broad stakeholder support; aligned with the behavioural literature discussed in Chapter 2,	Low	12-24 months

Rank	Policy Measure	Mean Support (1-5)	Key Evidence and Rationale	Estimated Cost	Indicative Timeframe
			especially regarding participation inertia and the value of default mechanisms.		
4	Public-private system integration	4.01	Positively associated with respondents' broader support for diversification and a more coherent multi-pillar pension structure, making it relevant for long-term system legitimacy and coordination.	Medium	2-3 years
5	Strengthened EU/EIOPA cross-border frameworks	4.09	Respondents support a stronger role for EU/EIOPA in ensuring fair pension provision (M = 4.09); this supports broader governance credibility and possible cross-border development pathways.	Low	12 months

The ranking suggests that stakeholders favour a reform path that combines participation incentives with trust-building measures. In particular, tax incentives and stronger consumer protection emerge as the most immediately actionable priorities, while broader public-private integration and stronger cross-border regulatory coordination appear more medium-term in nature.

The policy recommendations emerging from this research should not be understood as a uniform package of equal urgency. Rather, the findings suggest a hierarchy of measures that differ in immediacy, implementation complexity, and likely institutional impact. As Table 5.2 shows, respondents place the strongest overall support behind tax incentives and stronger consumer protection, indicating that participation and trust must be addressed simultaneously if supplementary pensions are to expand in a socially legitimate way. Tax incentives appear particularly relevant as a medium-term participation lever, while stronger consumer protection can be implemented more quickly and may help address the credibility deficit reflected in the low assessment of current government support. Auto-enrolment represents a particularly important behavioural instrument, as it can reduce participation inertia without requiring fully active decision-making by all households. By contrast, deeper public-private integration and stronger EU/EIOPA-related coordination are more medium-term reforms that depend on broader institutional alignment. Taken together, these priorities suggest that pension reform in Greece should proceed in sequenced stages: first by strengthening trust and participation conditions, then by embedding supplementary provision more firmly within a coherent multi-pillar governance framework.

From an implementation perspective, responsibility for these measures is distributed across different actor groups. Policymakers should take the lead on tax reform, auto-enrolment design, and the legal framework for consumer protection. Supervisory authorities should focus on disclosure standards, fee transparency, and the oversight of product fairness. Private insurers, in turn, should respond by developing simpler and more transparent retirement products that align with the expectations identified in the survey. This division of responsibilities is important because it shows that supplementary pension expansion cannot be driven by market actors alone; it requires coordinated action between the state, regulators, and providers.

5.8 Future Research

While this research project has provided significant insights into the sustainability and adequacy of Greece's pension system, there are several important areas where future research could build upon the findings presented here. These areas offer opportunities to further explore the complexities of pension systems in Greece and beyond, especially in light of the demographic and economic challenges facing many countries today.

Long-Term Impact of Auto-Enrolment on Pension Adequacy: One of the key recommendations from this study is the introduction of auto-enrolment for supplementary pension schemes. While this policy has been widely successful in countries like the UK, its long-term impact on pension adequacy in Greece remains to be fully understood. Future research could investigate the long-term effects of auto-enrolment on pension system sustainability, particularly focusing on how this policy influences the retirement savings behavior of younger populations. Additionally, it would be valuable to examine whether opt-out rates change over time and how auto-enrolment influences individuals' perceptions of pension products.

Cross-Border Pension Solutions: Given the increasing globalization of the labour market, cross-border pension solutions, such as the Pan-European Personal Pension Product (PEPP), are likely to become more relevant for Greece as its pension system continues to evolve. Future research could explore the effectiveness of cross-border pension solutions in helping countries with ageing populations diversify their pension systems. This research could assess how cross-border pension options might be integrated into Greece's existing multi-pillar system and the potential regulatory challenges associated with cross-border pension schemes.

Role of Technology in Pension Management: The role of technology in pension management has been rapidly evolving, particularly in the areas of financial planning, investment management, and administrative efficiency. Future research could examine how financial technologies (FinTech), such as digital platforms for pension management, robo-advisors, and blockchain-based pension products, could improve efficiency, transparency, and accessibility within the Greek pension system. Additionally, studying the integration of digital solutions into pension schemes could provide insights into their impact on participation rates and consumer engagement, especially among younger generations who are more tech-savvy.

Economic Shocks and Pension System Resilience: This research has primarily focused on the demographic pressures affecting Greece's pension system. However, the impact of economic downturns or political instability on pension system resilience has not been fully explored. Given Greece's economic history, particularly during the financial crisis of the late 2000s, future research could investigate how economic recessions or austerity measures influence the sustainability and adequacy of pension systems. It would be important to understand how such shocks affect both public and private pension schemes, and whether adjustments can be made to improve system resilience in times of economic distress.

Consumer Behavior and Trust in Pension Products: While this dissertation has provided insights into the importance of consumer protection and transparency in pension products, there is a need for further research into consumer behavior and trust in private pension schemes. Future studies could explore the psychological factors that influence individuals' decisions to participate in pension schemes, particularly focusing on trust in the financial industry and the perceived risk associated with private pension products. Additionally, qualitative research could provide a deeper understanding of consumer attitudes towards pension savings and identify barriers to participation, especially among younger or lower-income populations.

Gender and Pension Adequacy: An important area for future research is the gender gap in pension savings. Although not directly addressed in this study, it is widely known that women tend to accumulate fewer pension savings than men, due to factors like career breaks, lower lifetime earnings, and longer life expectancies. Future research could investigate the gendered impact of pension reforms in Greece and how public and private pension systems can be designed or adjusted to address gender disparities in retirement savings.

A further area for future research concerns the practical sequencing of pension reform measures in Greece. This thesis has shown that stakeholders support a combination of tax incentives, consumer protection, auto-enrolment, and stronger integration between public and private pillars. Future research could therefore examine which of these measures should be introduced first and which combinations are most likely to produce lasting participation effects. This would be particularly useful in the Greek context, where reform success may depend not only on the quality of individual policy instruments, but also on the order in which they are implemented.

Another useful direction would be more detailed research on different stakeholder groups. The present study included respondents from insurance, policy, academic, and related professional backgrounds, but future research could compare these groups more systematically. For example, it would be useful to know whether policymakers, insurers, and pension experts differ significantly in how they assess trust, adequacy, and the role of private providers. Such work could help clarify whether broad agreement exists across stakeholder categories, or whether support for supplementary pension expansion remains uneven across professional groups.

Future research could also make greater use of qualitative methods. While the survey approach used in this dissertation was useful for identifying broad patterns and associations, interviews or focus groups could provide a deeper understanding of how key actors interpret pension reform in practice. This would be especially valuable in relation to issues such as trust, regulatory credibility, and household reluctance to engage with long-term financial products. In the Greek case, qualitative evidence could help explain why certain reforms appear attractive in principle but may face difficulties in implementation or public acceptance.

A related area for further study concerns the difference between stakeholder perceptions and actual household behaviour. This dissertation shows that respondents see supplementary pension provision as increasingly relevant, but this does not necessarily mean that households will participate at the expected scale. Future research could therefore combine survey evidence with household-level data on saving behaviour, pension-product uptake, or contribution patterns. Such work would make it possible to test whether the views expressed by experts and practitioners are reflected in real participation outcomes.

Finally, future research could examine the Greek case in a broader Southern European perspective. Greece shares a number of structural features with countries such as Italy, Spain, and Portugal, including population ageing, high public pension dependence, and pressure to diversify retirement income sources. Comparative research across these systems could help identify which policy designs are more transferable and which institutional differences matter most. This would not only strengthen the comparative relevance of the present study, but also provide a clearer basis for judging whether the Greek pension challenge is exceptional or part of a wider regional pattern.

5.9 Final Reflection

This dissertation has shown that pension reform in Greece is more complex than a narrow discussion of fiscal sustainability might suggest. The issue is not only how to contain long-term public expenditure, but also how to maintain adequacy, trust, and institutional legitimacy in a system that has already been shaped by repeated reform and economic disruption. Looking back on the research as a whole, one of the clearest conclusions is that demographic pressure, governance, and public confidence cannot be treated as separate issues.

A second point that emerged from the study is that the possible role of private insurers needs to be interpreted carefully. The findings do not support the idea that private provision can replace the public pension system in any straightforward way. They point instead to a more limited but still important role, especially where supplementary products are transparent, well governed, and clearly positioned as complements to public provision. In the Greek case, this distinction matters, because trust remains fragile and any reform perceived as simple retrenchment is likely to face resistance.

The research process also made the value and the limits of stakeholder-based evidence more visible. Gathering the views of respondents with professional exposure to pension and insurance issues helped clarify how sustainability pressures and reform options are understood in practice. At the same time, the study does not claim more than the evidence allows. Perceptions can illuminate reform feasibility and institutional priorities, but they cannot substitute for actuarial modelling, household-level behavioural data, or longer-term comparative research. This is an important qualification and should remain part of how the findings are read.

Another useful lesson concerns the interpretation of mixed empirical results. Not every finding was equally strong, and some statistical relationships were weaker than others. That does not make them irrelevant.

In an applied dissertation, even limited or non-significant findings can still be informative, especially where they point to uncertainty, disagreement, or institutional constraints that deserve closer examination. In that sense, the study has reinforced the importance of cautious interpretation rather than overstatement.

Overall, the dissertation supports a balanced view of pension reform in Greece. Long-term sustainability is unlikely to be secured through fiscal adjustment alone, but neither can it be addressed through market expansion by itself. The more realistic path appears to lie in a better governed multi-pillar structure in which the public system remains central, while supplementary provision develops under conditions of transparency, consumer protection, and policy consistency. This does not amount to a simple solution, but it does provide a clearer basis for thinking about how retirement security may be strengthened in an ageing society.

A key implication of this study is that reform measures cannot be judged only by whether they appear technically sound. At the beginning of the research, it was easy to think mainly in terms of policy tools such as tax incentives, funded products, or regulatory adjustments. However, the findings suggest that these measures only become effective when they are accepted by stakeholders, understood by households, and supported by a framework that is seen as fair and trustworthy. This has made me appreciate more strongly the value of applied research, because it shows that good policy is not only about identifying what is economically desirable, but also about understanding what is institutionally realistic and socially acceptable in a specific national context.

5.10 Practitioner Reflections: Open-Ended Research Dimensions

The quantitative findings presented in this dissertation address specific, measurable relationships between demographic pressure, pension adequacy, and the perceived role of private insurers. However, a number of qualitative dimensions cannot be fully captured through survey items alone. This section draws on the empirical results, the practitioner literature, and the author's professional experience in the insurance sector to provide a reflective synthesis addressing four substantive questions that extend beyond the statistical analysis: what systemic changes are necessary for Greece's pension system to remain financially viable; what role private insurers are realistically positioned to play in the future; how public trust in supplementary pension products can be rebuilt; and what structural barriers continue to constrain the expansion of supplementary pension provision in Greece. Together, these reflections are intended to complement the quantitative findings and to provide the practice-oriented perspective that applied doctoral research demands.

Necessary changes for long-term financial sustainability

The survey findings confirm that respondents hold limited confidence in the current Greek pension system's ability to ensure long-term sustainability, with a mean sustainability rating of 2.53 on a five-point scale. This finding is consistent with broader structural evidence: Greece's old-age dependency ratio is projected to increase substantially through 2050, while its pay-as-you-go architecture continues to concentrate risk within a fiscally constrained public pillar. Against this backdrop, three categories of systemic change emerge as prerequisites for long-term viability.

First, Greece must restructure its pension financing architecture by progressively diversifying away from sole reliance on contribution revenues. The high correlation between perceived demographic pressure and support for income diversification ($r = 0.488$, $p < 0.01$) demonstrates that practitioners already associate ageing dynamics with a structural need for multi-source financing. A credible diversification strategy would entail not simply adding supplementary pillars, but redesigning the fiscal relationship between public, occupational, and individual provision. In practical terms, this requires medium-term contribution reform aligned with actuarial projections, not only short-term fiscal adjustments.

Second, tax incentive reform is essential. The survey item on tax reform received one of the highest mean scores in the dataset (4.24), and its strong positive correlation with support for private insurance ($r = 0.537$, $p < 0.01$) suggests that practitioners view tax policy as a key enabling mechanism for supplementary provision. Greece's current incentive structure for private pension savings remains underdeveloped relative to comparable EU member states. A reform that introduces meaningful, accessible, and well-communicated tax advantages for individual pension contributions would substantially lower the participation barrier for working-age households, particularly those in middle-income segments who are currently underserved by occupational schemes.

Third, and perhaps most fundamentally, pension governance must be strengthened. The findings show that support for private insurer involvement is closely conditioned on governance quality, transparency, and consumer protection. Without credible institutional oversight, the systemic changes described above risk being technically sound but socially ineffective. Governance reform is therefore not a secondary consideration; it is a precondition for any other structural change to gain legitimacy and traction within Greek society.

The realistic future role of private insurers

The survey data support a conditional but substantive role for private insurers in the future of Greek pension provision. Respondents assigned high importance to insurer involvement (mean = 4.01) and particularly to the design of simple, transparent products (mean = 4.43). Yet this support is explicitly conditional rather than categorical. The regression results, while modest in explanatory power, confirm that perceived insurer importance functions as a significant predictor of supplementary pension support when governance quality is assumed. From a practitioner perspective, this conditionality is both realistic and appropriate.

Over a ten to twenty-year horizon, private insurers are most realistically positioned to serve three functions within the Greek pension architecture.

The first is longevity risk management. As life expectancy increases and the adequacy of public replacement rates declines, the demand for deferred annuities and longevity-linked products will grow among households that have accumulated savings through employment but face uncertain post-retirement income. Greek insurers, currently constrained by low market penetration and limited product diversity, will need to develop actuarially robust and affordable longevity products if they are to meet this demand credibly.

The second function is adequacy gap coverage for the self-employed and non-standard workers, groups that are structurally underserved by occupational schemes and who constitute a significant proportion of the Greek labour force. Individual pension insurance products, if appropriately designed and incentivised, could serve as a first entry point into supplementary provision for these populations. The third function is as a distribution and education channel. Given the low financial literacy around pension products in Greece, insurers with direct client relationships are well positioned to serve as intermediaries between regulatory frameworks and individual savers, provided that this role is conducted with genuine transparency rather than as a commercial exercise in product promotion.

Rebuilding public trust in supplementary pension products

The trust dimension is one of the most consistently important themes across the empirical findings. The strong endorsement for consumer protection legislation (mean = 4.25), product simplicity and transparency (mean = 4.43), and EIOPA oversight (mean = 4.09) all point to a stakeholder environment in which institutional credibility is perceived as fragile and in need of active reconstruction. This is not surprising given Greece's recent history of pension cuts, contribution increases, and repeated reform reversals, which have understandably generated scepticism about the reliability of long-term retirement promises.

Rebuilding trust requires action on at least three levels. At the product level, insurers must commit to eliminating the complexity and opacity that have historically made pension products difficult to evaluate for non-specialist households. Standardised disclosure formats, clear fee structures, and independently verified performance data are minimum requirements rather than optional enhancements. At the regulatory level, strengthening the supervisory capacity of the Hellenic Capital Market Commission and ensuring close coordination with EIOPA would provide the external accountability signal that markets alone cannot generate. At the political level, a cross-party commitment to pension reform stability over at least one parliamentary cycle would be necessary to credibly signal that supplementary provision will not be undermined by future fiscal emergencies.

From a practitioner standpoint, it is also worth noting that trust is rebuilt incrementally through experience rather than through communication campaigns alone. Early positive experiences with supplementary products, particularly when losses are avoided and returns are modest but reliable, are more effective trust-building mechanisms than any regulatory initiative or marketing effort. This places particular responsibility on insurers to prioritise product quality and long-term client relationships over short-term premium revenue.

Main barriers to the expansion of supplementary pension provision

Despite the broadly favourable attitudes toward supplementary pension expansion observed in the survey, the findings also reveal several structural barriers that limit the realistic pace of development. The most statistically notable is the low demand perception, with the survey item on sufficient market demand returning the lowest mean in the dataset (2.87) and the highest standard deviation (1.211), indicating considerable disagreement among respondents. This combination of low central tendency and high variance is itself informative: it suggests that practitioners do not share a common understanding of whether Greece currently possesses the preconditions for viable supplementary market growth.

Four barriers stand out as particularly consequential. First, income constraints limit savings capacity across large segments of the Greek working population. Households that have experienced wage compression, high unemployment, and irregular employment over the past decade retain limited disposable income for voluntary pension contributions, regardless of the attractiveness of available products. Second, financial literacy gaps reduce the ability of potential savers to evaluate pension products, compare providers, or understand the long-term implications of contribution decisions. These gaps are not uniform across the population; they are concentrated among younger cohorts, lower-income households, and self-employed individuals, precisely the groups most in need of supplementary coverage.

Third, regulatory fragmentation between public pension administration, private insurance supervision, and capital market regulation creates coordination costs that slow product development and increase compliance uncertainty for insurers. Without a clearer and more integrated regulatory framework, the commercial case for investing in product innovation in the Greek supplementary market remains weak. Fourth, and perhaps most behaviourally fundamental, present-bias and inertia remain powerful constraints on voluntary pension saving across all income levels. Even households with sufficient disposable income and adequate financial literacy frequently fail to initiate supplementary saving in the absence of strong default or auto-enrolment mechanisms. The survey's relatively strong support for auto-enrolment (mean = 3.93) reflects an implicit practitioner recognition that voluntary participation alone is unlikely to drive significant market growth within a reasonable timeframe.

Taken together, these reflections reinforce the core conclusion of the dissertation: that the future of Greece's pension system cannot be secured through any single institutional actor, policy instrument, or reform cycle. What is required is a sustained, multi-dimensional effort that addresses structural sustainability, insurer capability, consumer trust, and market barriers simultaneously. The practitioner perspective adds to the quantitative analysis by grounding these conclusions in the institutional and behavioural realities that empirical surveys cannot fully capture, and by affirming that the path to a more resilient Greek pension architecture is both necessary and achievable, albeit demanding in its prerequisites.

5.11 Bridge to Conclusion

The central issue addressed in this dissertation is how Greece can maintain pension adequacy in the face of sustained demographic ageing and limited fiscal flexibility. The evidence presented does not point to a single reform instrument or institutional actor as a solution. Instead, it indicates that the pension question in Greece is shaped by structural pressures that evolve over time and require coordinated responses.

The role of private insurers must therefore be understood within these constraints. The findings do not justify a replacement of public provision, nor do they suggest that market expansion alone would stabilise the system. What emerges instead is a more conditional picture: supplementary insurance-based provision appears relevant where regulatory clarity, consumer protection, and institutional credibility are present. Without these elements, expansion remains limited.

For this reason, the Greek pension debate cannot be framed simply as a choice between public and private models. The more realistic interpretation is that sustainability and adequacy depend on how different pillars interact under demographic and institutional pressure.

The overall conclusion of the study is that the Greek pension challenge should not be understood as a temporary fiscal problem, but as a long-term structural issue shaped by demographic ageing, institutional design, and public confidence. The evidence presented in this dissertation suggests that the sustainability pressures facing the public pension system are closely connected to concerns about future adequacy. In other words, the issue is not only whether the system can continue to finance pensions, but also whether it can continue to provide retirement income at a level that is socially acceptable and politically sustainable. This makes the Greek case especially important, because it illustrates how sustainability and adequacy cannot be treated as separate reform questions.

A further conclusion is that private insurers can make a meaningful contribution to the future development of the Greek pension system, but only under specific conditions. The findings do not support a simple shift from public provision to market-based solutions. Instead, they suggest that private insurers are most likely to play a constructive role when they operate within a framework of transparency, fair consumer protection, and strong regulatory oversight. This means that the expansion of supplementary pension provision depends not only on product availability, but also on whether households perceive such products as understandable, trustworthy, and relevant to their long-term retirement needs. In this respect, the study points to the importance of governance and legitimacy as central conditions of pension reform.

Finally, the dissertation suggests that the most realistic path forward for Greece lies in a more coherent multi-pillar approach. The public pension system is likely to remain the foundation of retirement income provision, but it will need to be supported by better-designed supplementary arrangements if future adequacy gaps are to be managed effectively. This implies that policymakers, regulators, and insurers should not be seen as acting in separate arenas, but as participants in a shared reform process. The wider contribution of this research therefore lies in showing that pension reform in Greece is not only a matter of financial adjustment, but also a matter of institutional coordination, public trust, and long-term social legitimacy.

Chapter 6 Implications for Other Ageing Societies

6.1 Introduction and Rationale

The preceding chapters have examined the sustainability and adequacy challenges of the Greek pension system and the potential role of private insurers within a multi-pillar framework. The findings, grounded in a stakeholder survey (N = 68), point to a coherent set of institutional and policy conditions under which supplementary funded provision can complement a reformed public pillar. This chapter extends the analytical scope of the study by examining whether, and to what degree, the lessons emerging from the Greek case carry relevance for other ageing societies.

The comparative exercise presented here is not primarily empirical. The survey data underpinning this dissertation are specific to the Greek institutional context, and no claim is made that the quantitative findings transfer directly to other systems. Instead, the chapter develops a structured conceptual comparison, drawing on published institutional data, OECD and EIOPA analyses, and the existing comparative pension literature to identify parallels and divergences between the Greek experience and three selected comparator countries: Italy, Portugal, and Germany.

The selection of these three cases is deliberate. Italy and Portugal share structural features with Greece that are well documented in the Southern European welfare state literature: high public pension dependence, historically generous entitlement structures, repeated reform under fiscal pressure, low insurance market penetration relative to northern EU peers, and pronounced demographic ageing combined with persistently low fertility. Germany offers a different institutional profile – a more developed supplementary pillar, greater insurance market depth, and stronger institutional capacity – but also faces sustainability pressures that make the Greek experience instructive from a different perspective. Together, the three cases allow the chapter to address both within-region transferability and cross-regime applicability.

The chapter is structured as follows. Section 6.2 examines the Italian case. Section 6.3 addresses Portugal. Section 6.4 considers Germany. Section 6.5 synthesises the comparative lessons and identifies a set of transferable policy implications emerging from the Greek experience.

6.2 Italy: Reform Under Fiscal Constraint

6.2.1 Structural Parallels with Greece

Italy represents perhaps the closest structural analogue to Greece among European pension systems. Both countries operate predominantly within a pay-as-you-go (PAYG) framework, both have historically recorded among the highest levels of pension expenditure relative to GDP in the European Union, and both have undergone sustained reform pressure over the past three decades. Eurostat data indicate that pension expenditure in Italy accounted for approximately 15.4% of GDP in 2022, compared to Greece's 14.5% and the EU average of 12.2% (Eurostat, 2025). The two systems share a structurally similar fiscal burden and a comparable dependence on contributions from a shrinking active workforce.

Demographically, Italy is among the most rapidly ageing societies in the EU. The OECD projects that Italy's old-age dependency ratio will exceed 65% by 2050, placing it among the most exposed European countries alongside Greece (OECD, 2024). Italy's total fertility rate stood at 1.24 in 2023, below Greece's already low figure of 1.35, implying a comparably severe long-run demographic pressure on its contribution base (Eurostat, 2025a). Life expectancy at birth in Italy remains among the highest in Europe, which extends the pension liability horizon and increases the importance of longevity risk management.

Italy's pension system has been reformed repeatedly since the early 1990s. The Dini reform of 1995 introduced a notional defined contribution (NDC) framework for workers entering the labour market from that year onwards, replacing the previous earnings-related formula with a system linking benefits more directly to lifetime contributions and expected longevity. The Fornero reform of 2011, introduced under international fiscal pressure, accelerated this transition, raised retirement ages, and tightened eligibility conditions. These measures broadly paralleled the reform trajectory observed in Greece, though Italy's NDC transition proceeded more gradually and without the external assistance conditionality that shaped Greek pension policy in the 2010s (Jessoula, 2012; European Commission, 2024).

6.2.2 The Supplementary Pillar: TFR, Fondi Pensione, and Limited Participation

Italy introduced a supplementary pension framework based on occupational pension funds (fondi pensione) and open pension funds managed by financial institutions, alongside individual pension plans (PIPs) offered by insurance companies. A distinctive feature of the Italian system is the Trattamento di Fine Rapporto (TFR), a mandatory severance pay mechanism that can be redirected into occupational pension funds upon an employee's consent. The TFR mechanism was explicitly designed to channel deferred labour income into funded supplementary provision and represents a structurally relevant policy instrument for mobilising pension savings without requiring additional household contributions.

Despite these institutional mechanisms, participation in supplementary pension provision in Italy remains limited relative to the scale of demographic and fiscal need. COVIP, the Italian supervisory authority for supplementary pensions, reports that approximately 9.5 million workers were enrolled in some form of supplementary scheme in 2023, representing roughly 35% of the active workforce (COVIP, 2024). Participation is significantly higher among male workers, full-time employees in large firms, and workers in northern regions, compared to women, part-time workers, and employees in the southern economy. These distributional patterns are directly relevant to the Greek discussion, where similar structural inequalities are likely to constrain any expansion of voluntary supplementary pension saving.

The Italian experience also highlights the limits of tax incentives as a participation driver in the absence of strong enrolment defaults. Italy's supplementary pension contributions benefit from favourable tax treatment, yet voluntary participation has grown slowly and unevenly. Research suggests that inertia, financial illiteracy, and distrust of financial institutions have constrained enrolment even where fiscal incentives are present (Fornero & Lusardi, 2017). This finding closely parallels the Greek stakeholder evidence examined in this study, where respondents assigned the highest priority to product simplicity and consumer protection rather than to financial incentives alone.

6.2.3 Lessons for Greece

The Italian case offers three instructive lessons for Greece. First, a notional defined contribution framework can improve the long-run fiscal sustainability of the public pillar by aligning benefit levels with demographic and macroeconomic realities, but it does so partly by reducing replacement rates for future retirees. This creates an adequacy gap that supplementary funded provision must fill if pension income security is to be maintained. Greece's recent reforms and the introduction of TEKA point in a similar direction, and the Italian experience suggests that the adequacy gap will widen gradually rather than immediately, making early supplementary participation decisions particularly consequential.

Second, the TFR mechanism illustrates that supplementary pension mobilisation can draw on existing deferred compensation channels rather than requiring new household savings flows. Greece does not have an equivalent instrument at scale, but the principle of redirecting deferred labour income into funded schemes merits serious policy attention, particularly given low household saving capacity in the post-crisis environment.

Third, the Italian case demonstrates that voluntary participation frameworks, even when supported by favourable tax treatment, tend to produce unequal and limited coverage. The stakeholder survey evidence presented in this dissertation, which shows strong support for auto-enrolment (M = 3.93), is consistent with the conclusion that structured default mechanisms are likely to be necessary to achieve broad supplementary participation in Southern European institutional environments.

6.3 Portugal: Trust and Reform Credibility

6.3.1 Structural Parallels with Greece

Portugal shares with Greece a set of institutional and demographic features that make it a closely relevant comparator. Both countries operate predominantly PAYG public pension systems that have undergone sustained reform since the 2010s, both recorded pension expenditure significantly above the EU average during the post-crisis period, and both face pronounced long-run demographic ageing combined with high youth emigration that reduces the contributor base. Portugal's old-age dependency ratio stood at approximately 38% in 2024 and is projected by Eurostat to rise above 55% by 2050, a trajectory broadly comparable to Greece (Eurostat, 2023).

Portugal's pension system was substantially reformed under the 2011–2014 adjustment programme. Measures included benefit cuts, indexation changes, contribution base adjustments, and revisions to early retirement rules. The reform trajectory paralleled the Greek experience closely, though Portugal's institutional capacity enabled somewhat faster implementation. Post-crisis recovery has been stronger in Portugal than in Greece, and government debt-to-GDP has declined more rapidly, providing greater fiscal space for pension policy adjustments (European Commission, 2024).

The Portuguese insurance market is more developed than Greece's, with insurance penetration of approximately 3.8% of GDP in 2022 according to

EIOPA data, compared to Greece's 2.1%. Life insurance and pension savings products are more widely distributed in Portugal, though market depth remains well below northern European benchmarks. This difference in starting conditions is relevant for assessing the pace at which supplementary pension provision can realistically expand.

6.3.2 The Third Pillar and the Role of PPR Products

Portugal's third pillar is organised primarily around Planos Poupança Reforma (PPR), tax-advantaged individual savings plans managed by insurance companies, investment funds, or pension fund managers. PPR products have existed since the late 1980s and have accumulated a meaningful asset base over time, though participation remains concentrated among higher-income households. The Portuguese government has periodically adjusted the tax treatment of PPR contributions and redemptions to encourage longer-term accumulation, though these adjustments have sometimes created uncertainty about product terms and contributed to trust deficits among potential participants.

A distinctive challenge in Portugal, directly relevant to Greece, concerns the relationship between reform credibility and household saving behaviour. Research on Portuguese pension saving suggests that repeated adjustments to public pension parameters – including changes to indexation formulae, sustainability factors, and retirement age rules – have weakened households' confidence in the long-run value of supplementary pension contributions (Bravo et al., 2021). If households expect public pension rules to continue changing, they may rationally discount the value of locking savings into long-term pension products. This mechanism closely parallels the trust and credibility concerns identified in the Greek stakeholder survey, where low confidence in the long-term stability of pension arrangements was a recurrent theme.

6.3.3 Lessons for Greece

The Portuguese experience generates three specific lessons relevant to the Greek case. First, tax-advantaged individual savings products can create a third-pillar infrastructure relatively quickly, but their reach tends to be socially unequal unless complemented by stronger enrolment incentives or employer-based distribution channels. Greece's current third-pillar products face similar distributional constraints, and the stakeholder support for tax reform (M = 4.24) documented in this study reflects a broadly shared recognition that fiscal incentives are necessary but not sufficient for participation growth.

Second, reform credibility is a material determinant of household savings behaviour. Portugal's experience suggests that frequent adjustments to pension parameters – even when individually justified on fiscal grounds – can erode the perceived value of supplementary saving. Greece, which has undergone particularly intense and repeated reform, faces an especially acute version of this credibility challenge. The strong stakeholder support for consumer protection (M = 4.25) and simple product design (M = 4.43) in the Greek survey can be partly read as a response to this environment: households need institutional anchors they can trust in a setting where public pension rules have repeatedly changed.

Third, Portugal's relatively stronger post-crisis recovery illustrates that the conditions constraining supplementary pension development are not permanent. As fiscal space expands and institutional trust is gradually rebuilt, the conditions for supplementary pension growth can improve. This is a relevant perspective for Greece, where the current constraints on market development may be more contingent on the quality and consistency of policy over the coming decade than permanently structural

6.4 Germany: Institutional Depth and the Riester Paradox

6.4.1 A Different Institutional Profile

Germany represents a different kind of comparator. Its pension system is more institutionally developed than either Italy's or Portugal's, its supplementary pillar is considerably larger, and its insurance market depth – with insurance penetration exceeding 10% of GDP – is among the highest in Europe (EIOPA, 2024). Germany does not face the same acute adequacy gap or fiscal fragility that characterises the Southern European cases. However, the German experience is instructive for Greece precisely because of its more developed institutional framework: it illustrates both what a more mature supplementary pension system looks like and where even advanced systems encounter persistent limitations.

Germany's pension system rests on a statutory PAYG first pillar (gesetzliche Rentenversicherung) complemented by occupational second-pillar arrangements (betriebliche Altersversorgung) and state-subsidised individual retirement savings in the form of the Riester pension. The statutory system has undergone significant reform since 2001, including the introduction of a sustainability factor that automatically reduces benefit adjustments when the ratio of contributors to pensioners deteriorates, and a gradual increase in the standard retirement age to 67. These adjustments have improved the system's long-run fiscal position but have contributed to declining net replacement rates, particularly for lower-income workers with interrupted careers (Börsch-Supan & Wilke, 2004; OECD, 2024).

6.4.2 The Riester Paradox and Its Policy Lessons

The Riester pension was introduced in 2001 as a state-subsidised voluntary third-pillar product designed to compensate for declining public pension replacement rates. Take-up reached approximately 16 million contracts by the mid-2010s, making it the largest individually subscribed supplementary pension product in Europe at the time. However, participation has since stagnated and recently declined, with a significant share of contracts in a contribution-free or dormant status. A substantial academic literature has documented what has been described as the 'Riester paradox': despite relatively generous state subsidies, the product has been criticised for excessive complexity, high administrative costs, opaque fee structures, and limited portability, all of which have reduced its practical value, particularly for lower-income households (Börsch-Supan et al., 2012; Corneo et al., 2015).

The German experience is directly relevant to Greece for several reasons. It demonstrates, first, that state subsidies alone do not guarantee broad participation in voluntary supplementary pension products. Product complexity and cost opacity are barriers that fiscal incentives cannot easily overcome, particularly for households with limited financial literacy or limited disposable income. Second, it illustrates that voluntary third-pillar products tend to achieve greater coverage among higher-income, better-educated, and more financially confident households – precisely those who need supplementary provision least. Third, the Riester experience has prompted a broader policy debate in Germany about whether voluntary products should be complemented by automatic enrolment mechanisms, a debate that directly mirrors the policy discussion identified in the Greek stakeholder survey.

Germany's occupational pension sector offers a more positive reference point. Coverage has expanded substantially following legislative changes in 2002 and 2018, including the introduction of a right for employees to redirect employer contributions into occupational schemes and, more recently, elements of auto-enrolment in collective agreements. Employer-based distribution channels, integration with payroll systems, and collective bargaining have supported coverage in ways that voluntary market channels have not.

6.4.3 Lessons for Greece from the German Experience

Germany's experience generates three lessons relevant to Greece. First, it demonstrates that even relatively mature and well-resourced supplementary pension systems encounter persistent participation limitations when products are complex, costly, or difficult for ordinary households to evaluate. Greece should prioritise product simplicity and cost transparency from the outset rather than allowing a complex product landscape to develop that subsequently proves difficult to reform. The strong stakeholder consensus around simple and transparent product design (M = 4.43) in the Greek survey is consistent with this lesson.

Second, Germany's experience with its occupational pension sector suggests that employer-based distribution and collective enrolment mechanisms can achieve broader and more equitable coverage than individually sold products. For Greece, this implies that occupational pension development – building on the TEKA framework – deserves at least as much policy attention as the third-pillar individual market.

Third, the ongoing Riester reform debate in Germany illustrates that even well-established voluntary pension products can lose momentum and political legitimacy if they fail to deliver clear value to a broad cross-section of participants. This reinforces the case for considering auto-enrolment as part of the Greek reform agenda from an early stage rather than as a later corrective measure.

6.5 Synthesis: Transferable Lessons from the Greek Case

Having examined the three comparator cases, it is possible to identify a set of lessons flowing in both directions: lessons that the comparator countries offer Greece, and lessons that the Greek experience may offer to similarly positioned systems.

The most direct transferable lesson from Greece concerns the sequencing of trust and institutional reform. Greece's experience demonstrates that pension reform, even when fiscally necessary, can generate enduring trust deficits that constrain subsequent efforts to expand funded supplementary provision. Italy, Portugal, and to a lesser extent Germany all face variants of this challenge. The Greek stakeholder evidence suggests that credibility-building measures – strong consumer protection, transparent product disclosure, simple design standards, and effective regulatory oversight – should precede or accompany market expansion efforts rather than following them.

A second transferable lesson concerns the distributional limits of voluntary participation. All three comparator cases exhibit similar patterns of unequal participation: higher uptake among male, full-time, higher-income, and better-educated workers, and lower uptake among women, part-time workers, the self-employed, and workers in smaller enterprises. The Greek stakeholder evidence points in the same direction. Auto-enrolment, default mechanisms, and collective schemes appear to be necessary complements to voluntary frameworks across all four contexts.

A third transferable lesson concerns the role of private insurers. In each of the three comparator countries, insurance companies play a meaningful role in supplementary pension provision. The Greek evidence similarly identifies private insurers as potential contributors to adequacy and risk management, but emphasises that their credibility depends on governance quality, product transparency, and regulatory oversight. This finding is likely to be relevant across all four contexts: the value of private insurer involvement in supplementary pension systems depends critically on the quality of the regulatory framework within which they operate.

A fourth lesson, particularly instructive from the German case, concerns the danger of product complexity. The Riester experience illustrates that even generous subsidies cannot overcome the participation barriers created by opaque or difficult-to-understand products. Greece, Portugal, and Italy all have an opportunity to learn from this experience by building simpler, more transparent product standards into their supplementary pension frameworks from the outset.

Finally, the comparative analysis reinforces a conclusion already drawn in Chapter 5 of this dissertation: pension sustainability cannot be achieved through market expansion alone. All four countries face demographic and fiscal pressures that require coordinated action across public pillar reform, regulatory development, institutional capacity building, and supplementary market design. The Greek case is in some ways an extreme version of a common challenge – more acute demographically, more constrained fiscally, and more fragile institutionally than its comparators – but the structural logic is shared. The lessons emerging from the Greek experience, precisely because they were developed under severe constraint, may therefore carry particular instructive value for systems that will face similar pressures in less acute form in the coming decades.

6.6 Chapter Summary

This chapter has examined the pension sustainability and supplementary provision challenges of Italy, Portugal, and Germany in comparative perspective, drawing on published institutional data, OECD and EIOPA analyses, and the academic literature on pension reform in each country. The analysis has identified a set of structural parallels and divergences between these systems and the Greek case examined in this dissertation.

The Italian and Portuguese cases share the most direct structural parallels with Greece: high public pension dependence, pronounced demographic ageing, fiscal constraint, and limited but growing supplementary provision. Germany represents a more developed institutional benchmark that illustrates both the potential and the limitations of voluntary supplementary frameworks. In each case, the core lessons emerging from the Greek stakeholder evidence – the primacy of trust and institutional credibility, the limits of voluntary participation, the importance of product simplicity, and the necessity of governance quality as a precondition for private insurer involvement – prove to be broadly relevant.

The chapter does not claim that the Greek experience translates directly into policy prescriptions for other countries. Institutional histories, labour market structures, social contract expectations, and administrative capacities differ substantially across the four systems. What the comparative analysis does suggest is that the Greek case, precisely because it combines demographic severity, fiscal constraint, repeated reform, and low supplementary market development, provides a concentrated test of the conditions under which supplementary pension expansion succeeds or fails. The lessons drawn from this test are likely to retain analytical relevance for any society navigating the intersection of demographic change and pension system redesign.

Chapter 7 Conclusions

7.1 Overview

This chapter draws together the central findings, comparative insights, and policy implications of the study. It revisits the four research questions that have guided the analysis, synthesises the empirical evidence with the comparative observations developed in Chapter 6, and offers a final assessment of what the study contributes to the academic and policy literature on pension sustainability, supplementary provision, and the role of private insurers in ageing societies.

The chapter is deliberately concise. The empirical findings have been presented and discussed in detail in Chapter 4 and Chapter 5. The comparative analysis has been developed in Chapter 6. This chapter does not repeat those discussions but draws on them to construct a final synthesis that is both backward-looking, in the sense of consolidating what the study has established, and forward-looking, in the sense of identifying where the evidence points beyond its own boundaries.

7.2 Revisiting the Research Questions

The study was organised around four research questions. Each is addressed briefly below in light of the full body of evidence, including both the Greek stakeholder survey and the comparative analysis.

RQ1 asked how stakeholders perceive the long-term sustainability of the Greek pension system under demographic pressure. The evidence is unambiguous: sustainability confidence is low ($M = 2.53$), demographic pressure is recognised as the primary structural constraint ($M = 4.34$ and 4.31 for the two ageing-related items), and practitioners do not view the challenge as temporary or cyclical. The regression analysis indicates that ageing pressure was the only significant individual predictor in Model 1 ($B = -0.601$, $\beta = -0.344$, $p = 0.021$). However, the overall model explained only 11.3% of the variance in sustainability perceptions and narrowly missed conventional statistical significance ($R^2 = 0.113$, $F = 2.727$, $p = 0.051$). The result should therefore be interpreted cautiously as evidence that perceived ageing pressure is associated with lower sustainability confidence, rather than as a strong predictive model of pension sustainability perceptions. The comparative analysis in Chapter 6 reinforces this finding: Italy, Portugal, and Germany all face variants of the same demographic challenge, though with different institutional starting points and degrees of urgency.

RQ2 asked about the adequacy of the current Greek pension system and the risks of post-reform adequacy gaps. The mean adequacy rating of 2.28 indicates that respondents do not expect the current system to meet future retirement income needs. This concern is consistent with the structural trajectory identified in the literature review: repeated reform has improved fiscal sustainability indicators but has done so partly by reducing replacement rates, creating an adequacy gap that supplementary provision will need to fill over time. The adequacy gap is not unique to Greece: as shown in Chapter 6, Italy's NDC transition and Germany's declining statutory replacement rate present analogous dynamics, even if the severity differs.

RQ3 asked about the strategic role of private insurers in supplementary pension provision. Support for private insurer involvement is broadly positive ($M = 4.01$) but explicitly conditional. The highest-ranked item in the entire dataset is the need for simple and transparent product design ($M = 4.43$), followed by consumer protection legislation ($M = 4.25$). The regression analysis in Model 2 identifies perceived insurer importance as the strongest attitudinal correlate of support for the private insurance role in addressing adequacy gaps ($B = 0.546$, $p = 0.001$, $R^2 = 0.429$). This finding should be interpreted as evidence of attitudinal coherence rather than as proof of an independent causal effect.

This conditional endorsement is the study's most important empirical contribution: it establishes that practitioners see private insurers as credible only within a governance framework that prioritises transparency, product clarity, and consumer protection.

RQ4 asked about the policy measures required to expand supplementary pension provision. Tax reform (M = 4.24), consumer protection (M = 4.25), auto-enrolment (M = 3.93), and greater public-private integration (M = 4.01) all received strong support. The low internal consistency of the policy-related items ($\alpha = 0.400$) indicates that these instruments should not be treated as a unified policy-support scale. Rather, respondents appear to evaluate tax reform, consumer protection, auto-enrolment, and public-private integration as distinct reform instruments, a finding with direct implications for policy sequencing and communication.

The comparative perspective further supports this interpretation. The Italian, Portuguese, and German cases suggest that fiscal incentives alone are insufficient to drive broad supplementary participation, and that product quality, enrolment architecture, governance credibility, and institutional trust are at least as important as tax treatment.

7.3 The Central Argument: Complementarity Under Conditions

The study's central argument can be stated directly. Private insurers can make a meaningful contribution to retirement income security in Greece, but only under conditions that the market does not currently meet and the regulatory framework does not yet fully provide. Those conditions are governance quality, product transparency, consumer protection, and effective supervision. Where these conditions are present, supplementary funded provision can complement the reformed public pillar in a way that improves both sustainability and adequacy. Where they are absent, market expansion is likely to produce socially unequal, commercially shallow, and politically fragile results.

This argument is grounded in the empirical evidence, consistent with the comparative literature, and reinforced by the cross-country analysis in Chapter 6. It does not support the view that private provision can substitute for public pension reform, nor does it support a purely sceptical position that dismisses supplementary markets as irrelevant to the Greek context. Instead, it points to a coordinated reform logic in which the public pillar, the regulatory framework, and the supplementary market develop in tandem rather than in sequence.

7.4 Contributions of the Study

This study makes several contributions to the existing literature. First, it provides original empirical evidence on stakeholder perceptions of pension sustainability and the role of private insurers in Greece, a context that has been extensively studied at the macro level but less thoroughly examined through practitioner-level survey research. The N = 68 sample, while modest, is drawn from professionally relevant respondents across policymaking, insurance, and related fields, and the findings are methodologically grounded in a multi-method quantitative design.

Second, the study extends the multi-pillar literature by demonstrating, in an applied setting, the conditions under which practitioner support for funded supplementary provision is conditional rather than categorical. The finding that governance quality and product transparency are prioritised over financial incentives adds a dimension to the comparative pension literature that is sometimes underdeveloped in macro-level analyses focused primarily on replacement rates and asset accumulation.

Third, the comparative analysis in Chapter 6 situates the Greek case within a broader European and international framework, identifying transferable lessons that flow in both directions between Greece and its comparators. This comparative extension is a contribution specific to the present volume and goes beyond the scope of the original dissertation on which this publication is based.

Fourth, the study contributes to the applied DBA literature on pension governance by developing a set of concrete, actor-specific recommendations that are anchored in empirical evidence rather than derived purely from theoretical frameworks. The differentiation between recommendations for policymakers, private insurers, and regulatory bodies reflects a practice-oriented analytical approach consistent with the applied aims of doctoral business research.

7.5 Limitations and Boundaries of the Evidence

The study's conclusions should be read with its limitations clearly in mind. The sample size of 68 respondents, while appropriate for an exploratory stakeholder study, does not support broad statistical generalisation to all relevant actors in the Greek pension landscape. The sample over-represents insurance professionals relative to policymakers and public administrators, which may influence the direction of some findings. The survey captures perceptions and attitudes rather than observed behaviour, which means that expressed support for reform measures does not automatically translate into market uptake or policy feasibility.

The comparative analysis in Chapter 6 is conceptual rather than empirical. It draws on published institutional data and the academic literature rather than on original cross-national survey evidence, and it is therefore subject to the limitations of secondary source comparison. The three comparator countries, Italy, Portugal, and Germany, were selected for their structural relevance to the Greek case, but the selection is not exhaustive, and other comparators might yield different insights.

These limitations do not undermine the study's core findings, but they define the boundary within which those findings should be applied. The study is best read as a structured exploration of a complex reform environment rather than as a definitive assessment of Greek pension policy options.

7.6 Final Assessment

Greece faces a pension challenge that is both urgent and structurally complex. Demographic ageing is narrowing the contribution base, repeated reform has reduced replacement rates, fiscal space remains constrained, and institutional trust in long-term financial commitments is fragile. These conditions are not unique to Greece, but they are more acute in the Greek case than in most comparable European systems.

The evidence presented in this study does not offer a simple solution to this challenge. It does, however, point clearly to the conditions under which progress is possible. Those conditions include a governance framework that prioritises transparency and consumer protection, a regulatory environment that supports product simplicity and equitable access, and a policy approach that combines fiscal incentives with enrolment architecture rather than relying on either alone. The comparative experience of Italy, Portugal, and Germany confirms that these conditions are not self-generating: they require deliberate institutional investment and sustained policy commitment.

This dissertation does not argue that private insurers can resolve Greece's pension challenge. The evidence does not support that conclusion. What it does show is that a carefully governed, transparency-oriented supplementary tier can meaningfully complement the public system, and that the conditions under which this is possible are knowable, measurable, and to a significant degree achievable. The path forward requires coordinated action across institutional, regulatory, and market dimensions. It is neither straightforward nor guaranteed. But the evidence presented in this study, and the comparative perspective developed across its chapters, suggests that it is both necessary and, under the right conditions, realistic.

References

Ahmed, S. K. (2024). How to choose a sampling technique and determine sample size for research: A simplified guide for researchers. Oral Oncology Reports, 12, 100662. https://doi.org/10.1016/j.oor.2024.100662

Akter, S., Mahmood, A. K. A., Alsharkawy, A., Zakaria, H., Zainol, J., & Salam, A. (2025). Ethical principles in research involving human health. International Journal of Human and Health Sciences (IJHHS), 9(4), 197-199. https://doi.org/10.31344/ijhhs.v9i4.835

Alabbasi, A. M. A., Runco, M. A., Acar, S., & Jahrami, H. (2025). The reliability and validity of problem generation tests: A meta-analysis with implications for problem finding and creativity. International Journal of Educational Research Open, 9, 100472. https://doi.org/10.1016/j.ijedro.2025.100472

Ali, M., Kamil, N., Asjad, H. M. M., & Ejaz, S. (2025). Ethics and integrity: Essential pillars of research. BioScientific Review, 7(4), 01-06. https://doi.org/10.32350/bsr.74.01

Aligishiev, Z., & Blotevogel, R. (2025). No quick fix: The recovery and resilience plan and external position in Greece. Economic Modelling, 151, 107186. https://doi.org/10.1016/j.econmod.2025.107186

Bank of Greece. (2025). Occupational insurance funds: Total assets at end of Q2 2025. https://www.bankofgreece.gr/en/news-and-media/press-office/news-list/news?announcement=74e04640-0503-406f-8dc5-fbe744be9731

Bank of Greece. (2025a). Statistics on insurance corporations: Q2 2025. https://www.bankofgreece.gr/en/news-and-media/press-office/news-list/news?announcement=24954317-fe4f-4960-950a-b77d6911e348

Bell, E., Bryman, A., & Harley, B. (2022). Business research methods (6th ed.). Oxford University Press. https://doi.org/10.1093/hebz/9780198869443.001.0001

Bhandari, P. (2024, October 1). Ethical considerations in research: Types and examples. Scribbr. https://www.scribbr.com/methodology/research-ethics/

Borsch-Supan, A., & Wilke, C. B. (2004). The German public pension system: How it was, how it will be. NBER Working Paper No. 10525. National Bureau of Economic Research. https://doi.org/10.3386/w10525

Borsch-Supan, A., Bucher-Koenen, T., Coppola, M., & Lamla, B. (2015). Savings in times of demographic change: Lessons from the German experience. Journal of Economic Surveys, 29(4), 807-829. https://doi.org/10.1111/joes.12116

Borsch-Supan, A., Coppola, M., & Reil-Held, A. (2014). Germany: A mandatory defined contribution system? In N. Barr (Ed.), Evidence and innovation in housing law and policy (pp. 117–135). NBER Working Paper No. 19985. National Bureau of Economic Research. https://doi.org/10.3386/w19985

Bradburn, N. M., Sudman, S., & Wansink, B. (2004). Asking questions: The definitive guide to questionnaire design. John Wiley & Sons.

Corneo, G., Keese, M., & Schröder, C. (2010). The effect of saving subsidies on household saving: Evidence from Germany. Ruhr Economic Papers, 170. https://doi.org/10.2139/ssrn.1592453

Bravo, J. M., Ayuso, M., & Mekkaoui, N. E. (2025). Assessing the effectiveness of recent pension reforms: The French experiment. Socio-Economic Planning Sciences, 102, 102335. https://doi.org/10.1016/j.seps.2025.102335

Bravo, J. M., & Herce, J. A. (2022). Career breaks, broken pensions? Long-run effects of early and late-career unemployment spells on pension entitlements. Journal of Pension Economics and Finance, 21(2), 191–217. https://doi.org/10.1017/S1474747220000391

COVIP. (2024). Annual report on supplementary pensions in Italy 2023. Commissione di Vigilanza sui Fondi Pensione. https://www.covip.it

Chrysanthopoulou, X., Mavrommati, A., & Migdalas, A. (2023). Assessing the efficiency of occupational pension funds in Greece. Operational Research, 23(4). https://doi.org/10.1007/s12351-023-00807-4

Danchev, S., Gatopoulos, G., Kalavrezou, N., Mavropoulos, A., Pavlou, G., & Vettas, N. (2024). Equally poorer: Inequality and the Greek debt crisis. Fiscal Studies, 45(3), 359-375. https://doi.org/10.1111/1475-5890.12384

De Andres-Sanchez, J., & Puchades, L. G. (2025). Longevity risk and annuitisation decisions in the absence of special-rate life annuities. Risks, 13(2), 37. https://doi.org/10.3390/risks13020037

DeYoreo, M. (2018). Stratified random sampling. The SAGE Encyclopedia of Educational Research, Measurement, and Evaluation. https://doi.org/10.4135/9781506326139.n671

Dillman, D. A., Smyth, J. D., & Christian, L. M. (2014). Internet, phone, mail, and mixed-mode surveys (4th ed.). John Wiley & Sons. https://doi.org/10.1002/9781394260645

Dube, B., Nkomo, D., & Thokweng, M. A. (2024). Pragmatism: An essential philosophy for mixed methods research in education. International Journal of Research and Innovation in Social Science, VIII(III), 1001-1010. https://doi.org/10.47772/ijriss.2024.803073

Dushi, I., & Webb, A. (2004). Household annuitization decisions: Simulations and empirical analyses. Journal of Pension Economics and Finance, 3(2), 109-143. https://doi.org/10.1017/S1474747204001751

EIOPA. (2024). EIOPA staff paper on the future Pan-European Pension Product (PEPP). https://www.eiopa.europa.eu/publications/eiopa-staff-paper-future-pan-european-pension-product-pepp_en

EIOPA. (2025). Insurance stress test 2024. European Insurance and Occupational Pensions Authority. https://www.eiopa.europa.eu/insurance-stress-test-2024_en

Elder-Vass, D. (2022). Pragmatism, critical realism and the study of value. Journal of Critical Realism, 21(3), 261-287. https://doi.org/10.1080/14767430.2022.2049088

Elgeddawy, M., & Abouraia, M. (2024). Pragmatism as a research paradigm. European Conference on Research Methodology for Business and Management Studies, 23(1), 71-74. https://doi.org/10.34190/ecrm.23.1.2444

ELSTAT. (2024). Annual statistical data and analyses. Hellenic Statistical Authority. https://www.statistics.gr/documents/20181/eefc1fb0-8110-bb61-2746-612bdd92bf30

European Commission. (2023). Monitoring the level of financial literacy in the EU (Flash Eurobarometer 525). European Union. https://europa.eu/eurobarometer/surveys/detail/2953

European Commission. (2024). The 2024 ageing report: Economic and budgetary projections for the EU Member States (2022-2070) - Country fiche: Greece. Publications Office of the European Union. https://economy-finance.ec.europa.eu/publications/2024-

ageing-report-economic-and-budgetary-projections-eu-member-states-2022-2070_en

European Court of Auditors. (2025). Special report 14/2025: Developing supplementary pensions in the EU. Publications Office of the European Union. https://www.eca.europa.eu/en/publications/sr-2025-14

Eurostat. (2023). Population projections in the EU: Demographic future - a greying population. European Commission. https://ec.europa.eu/eurostat/statistics-explained/index.php?title=Population_projections_in_the_EU

Eurostat. (2024, May 3). EU life expectancy is estimated at 81.5 years in 2023. Eurostat. https://ec.europa.eu/eurostat/web/products-eurostat-news/w/ddn-20240503-2

Eurostat. (2024a). Demography 2024: Interactive publications. European Commission. https://ec.europa.eu/eurostat/web/interactive-publications/demography-2024

Eurostat. (2025). Social protection statistics - pension expenditure and pension beneficiaries. European Commission. https://ec.europa.eu/eurostat/statisticsexplained/index.php/Social_protection_statistics_-_pension_expenditure_and_pension_beneficiaries

Eurostat. (2025a). Fertility statistics. European Commission. https://ec.europa.eu/eurostat/statistics-explained/index.php?title=Fertility_statistics

Eurostat. (2025b). Government finance statistics. European Commission. https://ec.europa.eu/eurostat/statistics-explained/index.php?title=Government_finance_statistics

Feldstein, M. (2005). Structural reform of Social Security. Journal of Economic Perspectives, 19(2), 33-55. https://doi.org/10.1257/0895330054048731

Fornero, E., & Lusardi, A. (2017). Adequate saving for old age? The role of information and financial literacy. Journal of Pension Economics and Finance, 16(3), 358–372. https://doi.org/10.1017/S1474747216000275

Foster, C. (2023). Methodological pragmatism in educational research: From qualitative-quantitative to exploratory-confirmatory distinctions. International Journal of Research & Method in Education, 47(1), 4-19. https://doi.org/10.1080/1743727x.2023.2210063

Fowler, F. J. (2002). Survey research methods (6th ed.). SAGE Publications.

Glette-Iversen, I., Flage, R., & Aven, T. (2023). Extending and improving current frameworks for risk management and decision-making. Safety Science, 168, 106317. https://doi.org/10.1016/j.ssci.2023.106317

Guardiancich, I., & Natali, D. (2011). The EU and supplementary pensions: Instruments for integration and the market for occupational pensions in Europe. SSRN Electronic Journal. https://doi.org/10.2139/ssrn.2264143

Hanbali, H. (2024). Mean-variance longevity risk-sharing for annuity contracts. Insurance Mathematics and Economics, 120, 207-235. https://doi.org/10.1016/j.insmatheco.2024.12.001

Haynes, S. N., Richard, D. C. S., & Kubany, E. S. (1995). Content validity in psychological assessment: A functional approach to concepts and methods. Psychological Assessment, 7(3), 238-247. https://doi.org/10.1037/1040-3590.7.3.238

Hellenic Association of Insurance Companies. (2024). Greek insurance market statistics 2023. HAIC. https://www.eaee.gr/wp-content/uploads/2025/08/annual_stat_report_2023_eng.pdf

Hellenic Ministry of National Economy and Finance. (2025). Greece: Annual progress report 2025. https://minfin.gov.gr/wp-content/uploads/2025/04/Greece_Annual_Progress_Report_2025_300425.pdf

Holtom, B., Baruch, Y., Aguinis, H., & Ballinger, G. A. (2022). Survey response rates: Trends and a validity assessment framework. Human Relations, 75(8), 1560-1584. https://doi.org/10.1177/00187267211070769

Hossan, D., Wolfs, B., Jesmin, N. S., & Petkovic, M. (2025). Questionnaire validity and reliability: A review with practical guidelines. Journal of Entrepreneurship, Business and Economics, 13(1), 135-186.

International Monetary Fund (IMF). (2025). Greece: 2025 Article IV consultation (IMF Country Report No. 25/85). International Monetary Fund. https://www.imf.org/en/Publications/CR/Issues/2025/04/07/Greece-2025-Article-IV-Consultation-Press-Release-Staff-Report-and-Statement-by-the-Executive-Director-for-Greece-550338

Kalogeropoulos, K., Fragkopoulos, D., Andreopoulos, P., & Tragaki, A. (2024). Shifting sands: Examining and mapping the population structure of Greece through the last three censuses. Economies, 12(11), 294. https://doi.org/10.3390/economies12110294

Kangur, A., Kalavrezou, N., & Kim, D. (2021). Reforming the Greek pension system. IMF Working Papers. https://www.imf.org/media/files/publications/wp/2021/english/wpiea2021188-print-pdf.pdf

Jessoula, M. (2011). Italy: From Bismarckian pensions to multipillarization under adverse conditions. In B. Ebbinghaus (Ed.), The varieties of pension governance: Pension privatization in Europe (pp. 151–179). Oxford University Press.

Karnia, R. (2024). Importance of reliability and validity in research. Psychology and Behavioral Sciences, 13(6), 137-141. https://doi.org/10.11648/j.pbs.20241306.11

Kaushik, V., & Walsh, C. A. (2019). Pragmatism as a research paradigm and its implications for social work research. Social Sciences, 8(9), 255. https://doi.org/10.3390/socsci8090255

Kelly, L. M., & Cordeiro, M. (2020). Three principles of pragmatism for research on organizational processes. Methodological Innovations, 13(2). https://doi.org/10.1177/2059799120937242

Konstantinidou, D., & Koumarianos, E. (2025). Rethinking retirement in Greece: Flexible pathways, gaps and policy implications. Journal of Social Policy, 18(21), 29-50. https://doi.org/10.37509/socpol25182129k

Koo, M., & Yang, S. (2025). Likert-type scale. Encyclopedia, 5(1), 18. https://doi.org/10.3390/encyclopedia5010018

Kyriopoulos, I., Athanasakis, K., Tsoli, S., Mossialos, E., & Papanicolas, I. (2025). Addressing public health and health system challenges in Greece: Reform priorities in a changing landscape. The Lancet Public Health. https://doi.org/10.1016/S2468-2667(25)00188-4

Laliotis, I., Shaikh, M., Stavropoulou, C., & Kourouklis, D. (2023). Retirement and household expenditure in turbulent times. Journal of Family and Economic Issues, 44(4), 968-989. https://doi.org/10.1007/s10834-022-09884-7

Lavidas, K., Petropoulou, A., Papadakis, S., Apostolou, Z., Komis, V., Jimoyiannis, A., & Gialamas, V. (2022). Factors affecting response rates of the web survey with teachers. Computers, 11(9), 127. https://doi.org/10.3390/computers11090127

Lusardi, A. (2014). The economic importance of financial literacy: Theory and evidence. Journal of Economic Literature, 52(1), 5-44. https://doi.org/10.1257/jel.52.1.5

Lusardi, A., & Mitchell, O. S. (2014). How ordinary consumers make complex economic decisions: Financial literacy and retirement readiness. Quarterly Journal of Finance, 7(3), 1750008. https://doi.org/10.1142/S2010139217500082

Maier, C., Thatcher, J. B., Grover, V., & Dwivedi, Y. K. (2023). Cross-sectional research: A critical perspective, use cases, and recommendations for IS research. International Journal of Information Management, 70, 102625. https://doi.org/10.1016/j.ijinfomgt.2023.102625

Makantasi, E., & Valentis, H. (2024). Greece's economic odyssey: Persistent challenges and pathways forward. Economies, 12(6), 139. https://doi.org/10.3390/economies12060139

McCombes, S. (2023, June 22). Sampling methods: Types, techniques & examples. Scribbr. https://www.scribbr.com/methodology/sampling-methods/

Mills, J. G. (2025, January 25). How to conduct research with surveys: Definition and methods. SuperSurvey. https://www.supersurvey.com/Research

Munnell, A. H., & Soto, M. (2007). Why are companies freezing their pensions? Center for Retirement Research at Boston College Working Paper No. 2007-22. https://crr.bc.edu/working-papers/why-are-companies-freezing-their-pensions/

Myles, J. (2002). A new social contract for the elderly. In G. Esping-Andersen, D. Gallie, A. Hemerijck, & J. Myles (Eds.), Why we need a new welfare state (pp. 130-172). Oxford University Press.

Nektarios, M., & Tinios, P. (2019). The Greek pension reforms: Crises and NDC attempts awaiting completion. International Bank for Reconstruction and Development, Paper No. 1906. https://documents1.worldbank.org/curated/en/572351556878896140/pdf/The-Greek-Pension-Reforms-Crises-and-NDC-Attempts-Awaiting-Completion.pdf

Noble, H., & Smith, J. (2025). Ensuring validity and reliability in qualitative research. Evidence-Based Nursing, 28(4), e104232. https://doi.org/10.1136/ebnurs-2024-104232

OECD. (2015). Pensions at a glance 2015: OECD and G20 indicators. OECD Publishing. https://doi.org/10.1787/pension_glance-2015-en

OECD. (2017). Pensions at a glance 2017: OECD and G20 indicators. OECD Publishing. https://doi.org/10.1787/pension_glance-2017-en

OECD. (2020). OECD/INFE 2020 international survey of adult financial literacy. OECD. https://www.oecd.org/en/publications/oecd-infe-2020-international-survey-of-adult-financial-literacy_145f5607-en.html

OECD. (2024). Key policies to promote longer working lives: Country note - Greece. OECD. https://www.oecd.org/content/dam/oecd/en/publications/reports/2024/10/key-policies-to-promote-longer-working-live-country-notes_a9fc14ca/greece_03c59396/8132464b-en.pdf

OECD. (2024a). OECD Pensions Outlook 2024. https://doi.org/10.1787/51510909-en

Presser, S., Couper, M. P., Lessler, J. T., Martin, E., Martin, J., Rothgeb, J. M., & Singer, E. (2004). Methods for testing and evaluating survey questions. Public Opinion Quarterly, 68(1), 109-130. https://doi.org/10.1093/poq/nfh008

Rotschedl, J., Cermakova, K., Dick, T., & Pavelka, T. (2024). The sustainability of PAYG pension schemes: A comparative analysis (1993-2023). European Journal of Interdisciplinary Studies, 16(2), 25-51. https://doi.org/10.24818/ejis.2024.10

Setia, M. (2016). Methodology series module 3: Cross-sectional studies. Indian Journal of Dermatology, 61(3), 261. https://doi.org/10.4103/0019-5154.182410

Sharifnia, A. M., Kpormegbey, D. E., Thapa, D. K., & Cleary, M. (2025). A primer of data cleaning in quantitative research: Handling missing values and outliers. Journal of Advanced Nursing, 82(1), 970-975. https://doi.org/10.1111/jan.16908

Stathopoulos, K. K., & Vrontos, I. D. (2025). Macroeconomic factors and the life insurance sector in Greece: An analytical perspective. London School of Economics and Political Science, Hellenic Observatory. https://www.lse.ac.uk/Hellenic-Observatory/Assets/Documents/Events/2024-25/11th-HOC-PhD-Symposium-Papers-for-Publishing/A.3i.pdf

Tanko, F. (2024). Relevance of pragmatism as a philosophical perspective in social science research. SSRN Electronic Journal. https://doi.org/10.2139/ssrn.4956835

Tavakol, M., & Dennick, R. (2011). Making sense of Cronbach's alpha. International Journal of Medical Education, 2, 53-55. https://doi.org/10.5116/ijme.4dfb.8dfd

Thomas, L. (2023, June 22). Cross-sectional study: Definition, uses & examples. Scribbr. https://www.scribbr.com/methodology/cross-sectional-study/

Vittas, D. (2000). Pension reform and capital market development: Feasibility and impact preconditions. World Bank Policy Research Working Paper No. 2414. https://doi.org/10.1596/1813-9450-2414

Wan, C., Bateman, H., & Hanewald, K. (2025). Demand for life annuities, critical illness insurance, and long-term care insurance. Journal of Risk & Insurance, 92(3), 740-764. https://doi.org/10.1111/jori.70005

Wang, X., & Cheng, Z. (2020). Cross-sectional studies. CHEST Journal, 158(1), S65-S71. https://doi.org/10.1016/j.chest.2020.03.012

Willie, M. M. (2024). Population and target population in research methodology. Golden Ratio of Social Science and Education, 4(1), 75-79. https://doi.org/10.52970/grsse.v4i1.405

World Bank. (2020). Greece: Options for meeting the increasing demand for elderly care needs. World Bank Group. https://documents.worldbank.org/en/publication/documents-reports/documentdetail/793041593005209757

World Bank. (2023). World development indicators: Age dependency ratio, old. World Bank Group. https://data.worldbank.org/indicator/SP.POP.DPND.OL

World Bank. (2025). Old-age dependency ratio (% of working-age population) - Greece. World Bank. https://data.worldbank.org/indicator/SP.POP.DPND.OL?end=2024&locations=GR&start=1960

World Medical Association. (2024). World Medical Association Declaration of Helsinki. JAMA, 333(1), 71. https://doi.org/10.1001/jama.2024.21972

Appendix

Survey Questionnaire

Survey Introduction

Dear Participant,

Thank you for taking the time to participate in this survey, which is part of a research study conducted as part of a Doctor of Business Administration (DBA) dissertation. The purpose of this study is to examine the sustainability of Greece's pension system, particularly in the context of demographic ageing, fiscal constraints, and ongoing reforms. The research will focus on exploring the role of private insurers in contributing to Greece's pension system, with the aim of providing actionable insights for policymakers and insurance professionals.

As demographic pressures, economic conditions, and pension reforms continue to shape the future of retirement income in Greece, understanding the perspectives of stakeholders like yourself—whether you are involved in policymaking, insurance, or pension analysis—is crucial. This survey aims to gather your views on the current state of Greece's pension system, the challenges it faces, and the potential role of private insurance in supporting long-term sustainability and adequacy for future retirees.

All responses will remain confidential, and data will be anonymised for analysis purposes. The results will be used solely for academic research and will not be shared with third parties. Participation in this survey is voluntary, and you may withdraw at any time without any consequences. By completing this survey, you will be contributing to a better understanding of the challenges and opportunities surrounding Greece's pension system. Your insights will help inform practical recommendations for both public institutions and the private insurance sector.

Section 1: Demographic Information

1. **What is your profession?**
   - Policymaker
   - Insurance Professional
   - Pension Expert/Academic
   - Other (please specify)
2. **How many years of experience do you have in pension policy, insurance, or related fields?**
   - 0-5 years
   - 6-10 years
   - 11-20 years
   - 21+ years
3. **Have you previously worked with pension systems in Greece?**
   - Yes
   - No

Section 2: Perceptions on Greece's Pension System (pay-as-you-go Model)

4. **Greece's pension system is currently sustainable in the long term.**
   - Strongly Disagree | 1 | 2 | 3 | 4 | 5 | Strongly Agree
5. **The current pay-as-you-go pension system in Greece is adequate to meet the future needs of retirees.**
   - Strongly Disagree | 1 | 2 | 3 | 4 | 5 | Strongly Agree

6. **Greece's pension system is under significant pressure due to the ageing population.**
    - Strongly Disagree | 1 | 2 | 3 | 4 | 5 | Strongly Agree
7. **Demographic ageing will continue to strain Greece's pension system over the next 50 years.**
    - Strongly Disagree | 1 | 2 | 3 | 4 | 5 | Strongly Agree
8. **The current pension reforms will not be enough to ensure long-term sustainability.**
    - Strongly Disagree | 1 | 2 | 3 | 4 | 5 | Strongly Agree

Section 3: Private Insurance Role in Supplementary Pensions

9. **Private insurers can play an important role in supporting Greece's pension system.**
    - Strongly Disagree | 1 | 2 | 3 | 4 | 5 | Strongly Agree
10. **Private insurance products like annuities can help reduce the risk of outliving retirement savings.**
    - Strongly Disagree | 1 | 2 | 3 | 4 | 5 | Strongly Agree
11. **There is sufficient demand for supplementary pension products in Greece.**
    - Strongly Disagree | 1 | 2 | 3 | 4 | 5 | Strongly Agree
12. **Private insurers should focus on designing simple and transparent pension products for Greek citizens.**
    - Strongly Disagree | 1 | 2 | 3 | 4 | 5 | Strongly Agree

13. **The role of private insurers in pension provision is essential to reduce the pressure on the public pension system.**
    - Strongly Disagree | 1 | 2 | 3 | 4 | 5 | Strongly Agree
14. **Private insurers should focus on providing products that address longevity risks in the Greek pension system.**
    - Strongly Disagree | 1 | 2 | 3 | 4 | 5 | Strongly Agree

Section 4: Regulatory and Policy Environment

15. **The Greek government is doing enough to support the development of supplementary pension schemes.**
    - Strongly Disagree | 1 | 2 | 3 | 4 | 5 | Strongly Agree
16. **Greece needs to reform its tax incentives for private pension savings to increase participation.**
    - Strongly Disagree | 1 | 2 | 3 | 4 | 5 | Strongly Agree
17. **There should be greater integration between public and private pension systems to ensure retirement security.**
    - Strongly Disagree | 1 | 2 | 3 | 4 | 5 | Strongly Agree
18. **Policy measures such as auto-enrolment in supplementary pension schemes will help expand participation.**
    - Strongly Disagree | 1 | 2 | 3 | 4 | 5 | Strongly Agree
19. **Consumer protection laws should be strengthened to ensure that private pension products are fair and transparent.**
    - Strongly Disagree | 1 | 2 | 3 | 4 | 5 | Strongly Agree

20. **A Pan-European Personal Pension Product (PEPP) could provide a viable solution to Greece's supplementary pension challenges.**
    - Strongly Disagree | 1 | 2 | 3 | 4 | 5 | Strongly Agree
21. **The role of international regulatory bodies, such as the EU and EIOPA, should be enhanced to ensure fair pension provisions across Europe.**
    - Strongly Disagree | 1 | 2 | 3 | 4 | 5 | Strongly Agree

Section 5: General Views on Pension Reforms and Sustainability

22. **Greece should prioritize pension sustainability over short-term fiscal relief.**
    - Strongly Disagree | 1 | 2 | 3 | 4 | 5 | Strongly Agree
23. **Pension reforms should focus on ensuring that future retirees have adequate income despite demographic challenges.**
    - Strongly Disagree | 1 | 2 | 3 | 4 | 5 | Strongly Agree
24. **Greece's pension system needs to diversify its sources of retirement income to ensure long-term sustainability.**
    - Strongly Disagree | 1 | 2 | 3 | 4 | 5 | Strongly Agree
25. **The introduction of private insurance products will be essential to address future pension adequacy gaps in Greece.**
    - Strongly Disagree | 1 | 2 | 3 | 4 | 5 | Strongly Agree
26. **Greece should explore cross-border pension solutions within the EU to strengthen retirement income provision.**
    - Strongly Disagree | 1 | 2 | 3 | 4 | 5 | Strongly Agree

Section 6: The Future of the Pension System

27. What changes do you think will be necessary for it to remain financially sustainable and adequate for retirees?
28. What role do you see private insurers playing in the future of Greece's pension system?
29. What steps should Greece take to improve public trust in the pension system?
30. What are the main barriers to the expansion of supplementary pensions in Greece, and how can they be overcome?

Bridge to Comparative Analysis

This survey now includes 30 questions, with a mix of Likert scale and open-ended questions, focusing on various key aspects of the Greek pension system, private insurers' roles, and policy recommendations. The open-ended questions allow for deeper insights into respondents' perceptions, which will complement the quantitative data obtained from the Likert scale questions.

Bibliografische Information der Deutschen Nationalbibliothek: Die Deutsche Nationalbibliothek verzeichnet diese Publikation in der Deutschen Nationalbibliografie; detaillierte bibliografische Daten sind im Internet über dnb.dnb.de abrufbar.

Lektorat: Thomas Rammopoulos

Verlag: BoD · Books on Demand GmbH, Überseering 33, 22297 Hamburg, bod@bod.de
Druck: Libri Plureos GmbH, Friedensallee 273, 22763 Hamburg

ISBN: 978-3-6963-6809-8

FSC
www.fsc.org
MIX
Papier aus verantwortungsvollen Quellen
Paper from responsible sources
FSC® C105338